HEALING
AND
DELIVERANCE

A Present Reality

By Dr. Alan Pateman

BY DR. JENNIFER PATEMAN

AVAILABLE FROM APMI PUBLICATIONS, AMAZON.COM AND OTHER RETAIL OUTLETS

HEALING
AND
DELIVERANCE

A Present Reality

DR. ALAN PATEMAN

BOOK TITLE:
Healing and Deliverance, A Present Reality

WRITTEN BY Dr. ALAN PATEMAN
ISBN: 978-1-909132-80-1
eBook ISBN: 978-1-909132-81-8

Published By:
APMI Publications
In Partnership with Truth for the Journey Books **2**
Email: publications@alanpateman.com
www.AlanPatemanMinistries.com

Acknowledgements:
Author/Design/Senior Editor/Publisher: Apostle Dr. Alan Pateman
Editing/Proofreading/Research: Dr. Jennifer Pateman
Computer Administration/Office Manager: Dr. Dorothea Struhlik
Cover Image Credit: www.PosterMyWall.com

❖

Dedication

I'd like to dedicate this book to Doctor Ian and Rosemary Andrews who have been in the Healing Ministry for many many years.

I had the privilege of sitting under their ministry, where I gained experience in the things of the Holy Spirit and how to be equipped to heal the sick, which we are given as a commission from the Lord Jesus Christ: To go and preach the Gospel to every person and heal the sick... (Mark 16:15-18)

Ian Andrews is the Apostolic Director of The International Association of Healing Ministries and The International Apostolic Healing Institute.[1]

❖

Table of Contents

❖

Foreword

When Dr Alan Pateman first approached me about this book, **Healing and Deliverance, A Present Reality** my first reaction was - *"Not me! Why me?"* However, my next reaction is to say, *"Satan and your cohorts, take note, as God is, through this book, going to further expose your deception in holding down the 'sons of the King.'"*

I have known Dr Alan for quite some time now and have worked in cooperation and partnership with him and his ministry over these years.

My very first meeting with Dr Alan was in 1988, at a Larry Lea Prayer Conference in Nottingham. Ever since, God has drawn me closer to him and his ministry. The attraction has been my recognition under the Holy Spirit of the extraordinary prophetic anointing on his life, with an apostolic overtone, which has created an international demand for his ministry.

At times Dr Alan's prophetic, militant, aggressive, no-nonsense stance brings him into sharp focus in confrontation with "nice" Christians and even other leaders. He believes very strongly in coming against the devil and his evil cohorts in people's lives and throughout the nations. He is restless about taking the warfare to the devil's domain so that it can be repeatedly plundered and depopulated by aggressive prayer and warfare, backed up by a holy and righteous lifestyle.

The prophetic message he brings on DELIVERANCE is both clear and penetrating, but above all, down to earth. For too long Christians have only spoken about deliverance and in some circles has been marginalised and minimised, and ultimately, even born again, Spirit filled, tongue-blowing Christians have been allowed to continue under one bondage or deception of Satan or the other, the church living a defeated or defeatist lifestyle. In some cases, church leaders are terrified about the implications of the deliverance ministry and as such have held the ministry at arm's length through ignorance and fear.

The net results of such "niceness" and ignorance toward deliverance is that the church has suffered and the liberating message of deliverance has fallen into disrepute.

Within the pages of this book *(which has to be a "must-read" for any serious enquirer into the Healing and Deliverance*

Ministry), Alan unfolds a different pathway, so that the heartbeat of God's message of God's total deliverance can be released into the church of Jesus Christ today.

Dr Alan has expounded this message with a lot of skill, determination and passion that is borne out of much personal experience. He has indeed demonstrated clearly to us that our inheritance from our Father God is present deliverance from sin, sickness, disease, all bondages, fear, ignorance and even death!

Indeed, Healing and DELIVERANCE is a present reality!

Bishop Dr Ebi Edward Inatimi,
Senior Pastor of Toxteth Community Church, Liverpool
Director of INTERNATIONAL MINISTERS
EDUCATION PROGRAMME (IMEP)

❖

PART ONE

The Mystery
of Satan's Kingdom

❖

CHAPTER 1

His Origin

There is a force that is a present reality, which is actively working in the world today. This force is in direct opposition to the Kingdom of God. This force is the kingdom of darkness and is led by Satan, who is actively opposing and affecting the world systems: culture, media, government, economy, education, family, religion, politics, education, philosophy, entertainment and the arts.

This programme, which the enemy consistently carries out, is also directed at the bible believing churches with much hatred and brutality; his aim being to steal, kill and destroy *(John 10:10)*.

Scripture gives us information, which allows us, as followers of Jesus Christ, to recognise the enemy's attack in the world today.

If we are going to win the battle, we must know the enemy. We must not allow ourselves to remain in ignorance, but must acquaint ourselves with what the scriptures teach. Paul told the Corinthian church that Satan would have no advantage over us, for we will not be ignorant of his schemes.

In order that Satan might not outwit us. For we are not unaware of his schemes.

(2 Corinthians 2:11)

Poetic yet Mysterious

Michael Green gives us some background in his writings on Ezekiel 28. He says that this passage is like the passage in Revelation 12:9, "It needs to be treated with due caution. The language is poetic and the subject mysterious, but the main outline is as astonishing as it is clear."

The first ten verses of Ezekiel 28, speaks of the prince of Tyre, while the next nine verses speak of the king of Tyre.

Son of man, take up a lament concerning the king of Tyre and say to him: "This is what the Sovereign Lord says: 'You were the seal of perfection, full of wisdom and perfect in beauty. You were in Eden, the garden of God; every precious stone adorned you: carnelian, chrysolite and emerald, topaz, onyx and jasper, lapis lazuli, turquoise and beryl.

Your settings and mountings were made of gold; on the day you were created they were prepared. You were anointed as a guardian cherub, for so I ordained you. You were on the holy mount of God; you walked among the fiery stones. You were blameless in your ways from the day you were created till wickedness was found in you.

Through your widespread trade you were filled with violence, and you sinned. So I drove you in disgrace from the mount of God, and I expelled you, guardian cherub, from among the fiery stones. Your heart became proud on account of your beauty, and you corrupted your wisdom because of your splendor. So I threw you to the earth; I made a spectacle of you before kings.

(Ezekiel 28:12-17)

Such is the portrait of the one designated as king of Tyre. **Now for his lieutenant:**

The word of the Lord came to me: "Son of man, say to the ruler of Tyre, 'This is what the Sovereign Lord says: "'In the pride of your heart you say, 'I am a god; I sit on the throne of a god in the heart of the seas.' But you are a mere mortal and not a god, though you think you are as wise as a god.

Are you wiser than Daniel? Is no secret hidden from you? By your wisdom and understanding you have gained wealth for yourself and amassed gold and silver in your treasuries. By your great skill in trading you have increased your wealth, and because of your wealth your heart has grown proud.

"'Therefore this is what the Sovereign Lord says: 'Because you think you are wise, as wise as a god, I am going to bring foreigners against you, the most ruthless of nations; they will draw their swords against your beauty and

wisdom and pierce your shining splendour. They will bring you down to the pit, and you will die a violent death in the heart of the seas.

Will you then say 'I am a god,' in the presence of those who kill you? You will be but a mortal, not a god, in the hands of those who slay you. You will die the death of the uncircumcised at the hands of foreigners. I have spoken, declares the Sovereign Lord.'"

(Ezekiel 28:1-10)

Michael Green goes on to say that:

"The parallels are obvious. The charming, able, wealthy, prosperous prince of Tyre, so proud of himself, his achievements and his wisdom, will perish utterly, as a matter of fact he did. But behind the prince stood the king of Tyre, and the characteristics of the two of them are much the same. What concerns us here is the picture of the king.

He was originally in close intimacy with God. He dwelt on the holy mountain of God, he was an anointed cherub. He was blameless in all his ways, splendid in wisdom, skilful in his operation, perfect in beauty, the model of perfection.

Such was God's assessment of this magnificent creature, and note that he was a creature, *'On the day that you were created they were prepared' (Ezekiel 28:13)."*[1]

❖

CHAPTER 2

Pre-Adamic

S atan then, is not a grotesque monster with horns, as portrayed in the media. Satan, when he was created, was not evil. He *"had the seal of perfection"* and was *"full of wisdom and perfect in beauty."* His name originally was Lucifer, meaning *"bright and shining one"* *(Isaiah 14:12)*. He appears to have been one of the greatest of the angelic beings, but not for long because he FELL.

> *How you have fallen from heaven, o morning star, son of the dawn! You have been cast to the earth, you who once laid low the nations!*
>
> *(Isaiah 14:12)*

Pride was his Downfall

"God opposes the proud" *(James 4:6)*, pride of beauty, pride of position. Pride is the very thing that God hates, for in Proverbs 8:13 it says: *"I hate pride and arrogance!"*

Satan rebelled against God's will and decided to do his own will, for he said:

I will ascend to the heavens
- *Ambition*
I will raise my throne above the stars of God
- *Pride*
I will sit enthroned on my mount of assembly
- *Ambition in Ministry*
I will ascend above the tops of the clouds
- *Self-exaltation in Praise*
I will make myself like the Most High
- *Usurping another's Authority*
(Isaiah 14:12-14)

Because of this, God threw him out of Heaven:

I saw Satan fall like lightning from heaven.

(Luke 10:18)

The great dragon was hurled down — that ancient serpent called the devil, or Satan, who leads the whole world astray. He was hurled to the earth, and his angels with him.

(Revelation 12:9)

The World became Formless

In Genesis 1:1-2 (NKJV), it says: *"In the beginning God created the heavens and the earth. The earth was without form, and void; and darkness was on the face of the deep. And the Spirit of God was hovering over the face of the waters."* In the original translation it says, **"it became formless..."** If it "became," then it must mean that there was form before and there was some shape to it, there was an existence!

People often get confused about this because they see and think that this was the creation of the heaven and earth, and then life began. I believe the fall was before this time, and of course there is archaeological evidence to prove this *(fossils etc.)* It doesn't mention, for instance, dinosaurs going into the ark and yet we know from scripture that two from every type of creature went in *(Genesis 7)*.

We know from skeletons found by the archaeologists that dinosaurs indeed existed *(with various sources citing this period as 66 million years ago)*. There is also enough evidence in the scriptures to suggest that there was a prehistoric type of creation, which was destroyed by what we now know as the "ice age."

God created the earth billions of years ago and not just 6000 years ago, *(it has been 6000 years since Adam)*. We know through what scientists have discovered that the earth is much older than just 6000 years, therefore there must have been something before, something must have existed.

The Pre-adamic Time!

This pre-adamic time is where Satan existed and ruled, but at this time his name was still Lucifer, he did not become Satan until after the fall.

My people are fools; they do not know me. They are senseless children; they have no understanding. They are skilled in doing evil; they know not how to do good.

*I looked at the earth, and it was **formless and empty;** and at the heavens, and their light was gone. I looked at the mountains, and they were quaking; all the hills were swaying. I looked, and there were no people; every bird in the sky had flown away. I looked, and the fruitful land was a desert; all its towns lay in ruins before the Lord, before his fierce anger.*

*This is what the Lord says: "The whole land will be ruined, though **I will not destroy it completely.** Therefore the earth will mourn and the heavens above **grow dark,** because I have spoken and will not relent, I have decided and will not turn back."*

(Jeremiah 4:22-28)

I personally believe this scripture is talking about an existence of life before everything was laid bare, before the fall. Therefore, creation had to start all over again, we see this happening at the beginning of the bible.

In the Eternal Yesterday and the Ice Age

In Genesis 1:1 God said, *"In the beginning..."* the actual Hebrew translation says, *"In the eternal yesterday..."* In other words, it has always been; He is not someone who just turned up one day!

*He moves mountains without their knowing it and overturns them in his anger. He shakes the earth from its place and makes its pillars tremble. **He speaks to the sun and it does not shine;** he seals off the light of the stars. He alone stretches out the heavens and treads on the* *waves of the sea. He is the Maker of the Bear and Orion, the Pleiades and the constellations of the south.*

(Job 9:5-9)

So when God destroyed this planet, He sealed off the stars and the sun from this earth. If the sun is shut off what would happen? Everything on earth would freeze, this is how the ice age happened *(some scientists say that variations in the intensity and timing of heat from the sun are the most likely causes of the glacial/interglacial cycles).*

In Genesis 1:3 God then said, *"Let there be light."* **This "let" gives permission allowing it to come into being again.** It is not creative, just permissive. He permitted the light to shine once more.

Lucifer and a third of his angles were governing the earth, there was trading going on, there was life, there would have been creatures and some people. There would have been cities and all sorts of things going on, but this was all before the ice age, before the beginning as we know it.

Lucifer's Throne was in Eden

It was from here *(many sources say that Eden was in the region of Iraq)* that he controlled and gave orders. He governed the earth through the information he received from God.

He was not a man and he never had a position like Adam. He was not created for a relationship with God the way Adam was. He was created to minister to God and to carry out God's instruction here on earth.

Adam, on the other hand was given dominion over all the earth *(Genesis 1:26-28)*, but Satan through deception, was able to take this position from Adam. This gave Satan a **higher position** than he had ever held before his fall.

Satan had governed the earth, but fell from his position because of pride.

> *How you have fallen from heaven, morning star, son of the dawn! You have been cast down to the earth, you who once laid low the nations! You said in your heart, "I will ascend to the heavens; I will raise my throne above the stars of God; I will sit enthroned on the mount of assembly, on the utmost heights of Mount Zaphon. I will ascend above the tops of the clouds; I will make myself like the Most High."*
>
> *But you are brought down to the realm of the dead, to the depths of the pit. Those who see you stare at you, they ponder your fate: "Is this the man who shook the earth and made kingdoms tremble, the man who made the world a wilderness, who overthrew its cities and would not let his captives go home?"*
>
> *(Isaiah 14:12-17)*

We are the ones who will stare and ponder Satan's fate!

> *To him who loves us and has freed us from our sins by his blood, and has made us to be a kingdom and priests to serve his God and Father - to him be glory and power for ever and ever! Amen.*
>
> *(Revelation 1:5-6)*

Looking Down not Up!

Very often we think that Satan is pondering and looking down at us saying, "Hey, you people down there, do you know what is going to happen to you?" But no, it is not like that, it should be the other way around and we need to get an understanding of this.

And God raised us up with Christ and seated us with him
in the heavenly realms in Christ Jesus.
(Ephesians 2:6)

If we could just get hold of this simple revelation, that we are seated in the heavenly realms and that Satan is beneath our feet, it would cause us to stir ourselves up and see that we should be soaring above as kings, and as kings we should be looking down on Satan and **pondering his fate.**

But those who hope in the Lord will renew their strength.
They will soar on wings like eagles; they will run and not
grow weary, they will walk and not be faint.
(Isaiah 40:31)

It is important to remember also that Lucifer wasn't created evil but perfect *(Ezekiel 28:12-15)*. God gave him position, he was a guardian cherub and very beautiful. He fell because of his ambition, he tried to raise himself up higher than God, he became full of pride *(Ezekiel 28:17)*.

Responsibility of Leadership

Scripture tells us not to give "responsibility of leadership" to young converts. Why? Because young converts *(the spiritual immature)* who are given positions of authority, can easily become puffed up, as pride raises its ugly head. God says that we have to humble ourselves, then He will raise us up in due time *(1 Peter 5:6).*

There is nothing wrong with setting our eyes and minds upon the goal. It's important to be determined, to push through and to pull down the strongholds and deal with the things that hinder us.

We need to strive for our deliverance and seek God with all of our hearts and come into that place of unity, where we find perfect peace and growth. But to strive in the natural for position *(ambition),* is exactly what Satan did.

It is only God who is able to raise someone up into a position of ministry. There is no room for pride, because pride came before Satan's fall and it will come before ours!

> *You were anointed as a guardian cherub, for so I ordained you. You were on the holy mount of God; you walked among the fiery stones. You were blameless in your ways from the day you were created till wickedness was found in you.*
>
> *(Ezekiel 28:14-15)*

Satan was the one who was created to lead worship in heaven:

> *You were in Eden, the garden of God; every precious stone was your covering: The sardius, topaz, and diamond, beryl, onyx, and jasper, sapphire, turquoise, and emerald with gold. The workmanship of your timbrels and pipes was prepared for you on the day you were created.*
>
> *(Ezekiel 28:13 NKJV)*

Before his fall, Lucifer was a beautiful "being," with pipes coming out of him, his whole body was made up of musical instruments; everything about him, every gesture, was one of worship. This is the reason there is such a battle in society today over music. Music is the downfall of millions of people. If we don't understand and accept this, we are being deceived.

❖

CHAPTER 3

Ruler of the World

Jesus referred to Satan as *"the ruler of this world"* *(John 14:30 NKJV)*. In Ephesians 2:2 he is called, *"the prince of the power of the air"* *(NKJV)* and in 2 Corinthians 4:4, *"god of this world"* *(KJV)*, At the fall Adam and Eve, by yielding to Satan's temptations, sinned against God. Because of this we became fallen humanity, under satanic rule – slavery to sin *(Romans 6:17-18)*.

Before we met Jesus, we were under slavery to the world of darkness. We were being used to glorify Satan, but now because we have been touched by God, through our salvation and through the Blood of Christ, we are set free from the slavery which is upon the world.

For he hath made him [to be] sin for us, who knew no sin; that we might be made the righteousness of God in him.

(2 Corinthians 5:21 KJV)

"He offered Himself as a sacrifice on the cross. Being a sinless offering, and being a perfect man, He bore the judgement due to mankind through the breaking of God's law. Divine justice was satisfied through this once-for-all sacrifice.

Making it legally possible to receive the repentant sinner, not on the basis of his own righteousness, but because of the Blood of the Lord Jesus Christ, *(Matthew 26:28)*.

Our freedom from Satan's power, however, only becomes effective in our lives when we individually come to Jesus Christ by faith, confessing our sins and turning from our own way, and yielding to Him as Lord. Only then does His victory over Satan become our victory. How important it is to realise that because of His victory we have victory over the satanic influences. Apart from the Lord Jesus, we have no power to rise above spiritual forces of wickedness. Acts 4:12; Revelation 12:11."[1]

The Master of Disguises

Since the fall of Satan, these following names apply, they are names that clearly highlight his evil purposes:

Satan   -   Adversary [one who is hostile, opposing, against]   (Matthew 4:10; Zechariah 3:1)

Devil   -   Accuser, slanderer   (Matthew 4:1; John 8:44)

Serpent   -   A snake   (Genesis 3:1; Revelation 12:9)

Dragon   -   (Revelation 12:3-17)

Abaddon or Apollyon - Destroyer   (Revelation 9:11)

Belial   - Worthlessness, perverse   (2 Corinthians 6:15)

Beelzebub   - Lord of the flies, dung god of Ekronites

Enemy   -   (Matthew 13:39)

Adversary   -   (1 Peter 5:8)

Oppressor   - One who has dominion over   (Acts 10:38)

Accuser   -   (Revelation 12:10)

Murderer   - Destroyer of life   (John 8:44)

Liar   -   (John 8:44)

Roaring lion -   (1 Peter 5:8)

Deceiver   -   (Revelation 12:9; 2 Corinthians 11:3)

Prince of the power of the air   -   (Ephesians 2:2)

god of this world   -   (2 Corinthians 4:4)

Ruler of the world   -   (John 12:31, 14:30, 16:11)

Ruler of the demons -   (Matthew 12:24)

Tempter   -   (Matthew 4:3)

Wolf   -   (John 10:12)

Thief   -   (John 10:10)

Antichrist   -   (1 John 4:1-4; 2 John 7)

Angel of the abyss   -   (Revelation 9:11)

Condemner -   (1 Timothy 3:6)

Evil one   -   (Matthew 13:19)

King	-	(Revelation 9:11)
Trapper	-	(Psalm 91:3)
Angel of light	-	(2 Corinthians 11:14)
The Vanisher	-	I do not exist!

This is a lie that Satan provides for both the world and the church to believe. It seems that man would rather blame God for the evil that goes on in the world than seeing who is really behind it - Satan and his intelligence network.

Satan, unlike God, is NOT omnipresent; he is a created being, limited to being in one place at any time. He does, however, move about very freely *(Job 1:6-7)*.

An Angel of the Lord

Over the years there have been a number of people who have told me that they have experienced what seemed to be an angel of the Lord. But when they have gone on to describe what actually happened, what they were saying was not actually scriptural.

What the Lord revealed to me was that these spiritual experiences were in fact, not of Him or one of His angels but Satan's forces - masquerading as servants of righteousness.

For such people are false apostles, deceitful workers, masquerading as apostles of Christ. And no wonder, for Satan himself masquerades as an angel of light. It is not surprising, then, if his servants masquerade as servants of righteousness. Their end will be what their actions deserve.
(2 Corinthians 11:13-15)

On some occasions, after explaining to these people what the Word of God says, sadly some remain unconvinced and determined to believe that what they had seen was from God.

The Gift of Distinguishing

We know and see through scripture, the Lord and His angles have and still do appear to individuals. But we need to be careful. Yes, we can have many experiences as Spirit filled Christians but we need the gift of distinguishing of spirits *(1 Corinthians 12:10)*.

Even the elite can be deceived:

Watch out that you are not deceived. For many will come in my name, claiming, "I am he."

(Luke 21:8)

Paul in his instruction to Timothy says,

The Spirit clearly says that in later times some will abandon the faith and follow deceiving spirits and things taught by demons.

(1 Timothy 4:1)

We should treat these deceiving angels of light in the same way Smith Wigglesworth did when he awoke one night to find Satan standing at the foot of his bed. He said to Satan *"Oh it's only you,"* then turned over and went back to sleep!

❖

CHAPTER 4

Heavenly versus Demonic Music

Music is the most powerful force on the earth. Light travels at approximately 186,000 miles per second, travelling at such a high speed that it carries a threshold of audio-ability *(sound, being music or song)*.

The bible tells us: *"You are sons of the light..." (1 Thessalonians 5:5 NKJV)* God is light and in Him there is no darkness. We must live in the light. Focusing on negatives and insecurities equals darkness *(Romans 13:12; Ephesians 5:8; Philippians 2:15; 1 John 1:7)*.

Our worship unto Him is light:

What we see with our human visibility is about 3% of the light spectrum. Now, if God were to readjust our human visibility from 3% to 40% of the light spectrum, we would actually see our own worship *(worship being light)*. So, as we worship God, our worship *(light)* attacks the darkness and principalities and powers of the air, and completely drives them away.

Psalm 22:22 says,

I will declare your name to my people; in the assembly I will praise you.

Worship Dispels Darkness

So every time we worship God, Jesus comes into our midst and begins to praise His Father and as we worship the Lord, He not only hears our praises but sees them too! As we are worshipping God, our worship is actually dispelling the kingdom of darkness. As sons and daughters of the light *(1 Thessalonians 5:5)* we are worshipping the Father of Light, and that worship defeats Satan and his kingdom.

All your pomp has been brought down to the grave, along with the noise of your harps.

(Isaiah 14:11)

There is a battle going on in the world, as to who is going to get the praises. God wants His people to praise Him, but Satan wants himself to be lifted up in praise. He has a strong desire to be worshipped. Satan was thrown out of heaven because of this sin. I believe that as Christians we need to be extremely careful what music we listen to.

Reggae music is a major way of putting the Rastafarian message across. Rock music is also a way for Satan's influence to spread. Ray McCauley in recommending the book Bands Boppers and Believers says, "We all need to be informed and warned of the danger and threat that lurks behind the glitter and glamour of so many of these idols of pop music."

BANDS BOPPERS AND BELIEVERS takes a revealing look into areas of spiritual conflict, such as:

- Rude rhythms
- Music, moods and the mind
- Stars canvassing for cults and singing satanic songs
- The generation gap
- Peer pressure, the significance of which is seldom and insufficiently grasped in today's society

It is difficult when talking to young people about music, as you try to explain to them that music can either glorify God or glorify Satan, some just do not understand, or don't want to understand.

Music fell with Satan

Rob Mackenzie the author of the book, says on page 33 that, "He (Satan) began to desire worship for himself instead of being willing to give worship to God. As a result, Lucifer deceived one-third of the angels; and they were also cast out of heaven because of their pride. When Lucifer fell from heaven, **music fell with him.** Satan still has the ability to formulate, he desires worship for himself through music, and evidence strongly suggests that this is the motivating force behind a large portion of music we are hearing today."

He goes on to say *(page 45)* that, "Through the ages man has realised that music not only gives pleasure and enjoyment through listening, it has power to control our minds and bodies as well."[1]

Poets and the rest of us have long known about the link between music and mood, but "now researchers are plotting its links to long term health, mental balance and the possibility of moulding behaviour."[2]

Rob Mackenzie makes it quite clear that music does influence the listener, even if we are not aware of it.

"The body is constantly reacting to the sound, variations in pitch, rhythmic patterns, tempo and volume will affect pulse rate, blood pressure, respiration and the function of certain glands. These in turn will create a mood or elicit a physical response. Some music can make you relax and bring feelings of peace and contentment. Other music can cause frustration, nervousness or even depression."[3]

Creating an Emotional State

Dr Martyn Lloyd-Jones in his book, Preaching and Preachers, warns of the dangers that preachers can possibly make by directly attacking one's emotions or will.

He writes, "We can become drunk on music – there is no question about that. Music can have the effect of creating an emotional state in which the mind is no longer functioning as it should be, and no longer discriminating. I have known people to sing themselves into a state of intoxication without realising what they were doing."[4]

It is amazing when you look into the world of music, for we see rock stars leading thousands upon thousands of teenagers into the hands of Satan.

There are some rock stars like Elvis Presley who have been dead for years and yet are still worshipped. Shrines have been put up in his honour and he has become the poor man's guru.

Rob Mackenzie in his book brings out many **astonishing statements** *(page 15)*, which highlight our need to realise the importance of this subject.

- John Lennon is quoted as saying, "Christianity will go. It will vanish and shrink I needn't argue about that; I'm right and will be proven right. We're more popular than Jesus now."[5]

- David Wilkinson said, "Rock music is the biggest mass addiction in the world's history."[6]

Music a Mass Addiction

A personal testimony by Bill Dunn an Evangelist has been produced in tract form. He himself was involved for a period of time in the rock and roll scene. Names like Elvis Presley, Little Richard, Gerry Lee Lewis, began to impress him. He goes on to say the three things that surround rock music today are DRUGS, SEX and VIOLENCE. The heavy beat of some rock songs are a brain-washing formula which Satan himself is using to lure many to hell and a lost eternity.

Today in rock music there is what is known as "backward masking." This is where a song is put on record and a subliminal message is also put on in such a way that it cannot be heard by ear, but it is picked up through the subconscious mind, with such songs as "A Child is Coming."

Listening to the words, one would think it is a reference to the Nativity, the birth of Christ, but if you play the record in reverse the voice keeps repeating over and over in a brainwashing manner, "the son of Satan, the son of Satan!"

Many of the rock singers and groups are open worshippers of the devil and are involved in the occult.[7]

CHAPTER 5

Satan's Intelligence Network

We have discovered that Satan exists, and we have seen how he portrays himself. What we need to understand is that he has an organised army. *"For our struggle is not against flesh and blood, but against **the rulers**, against **the authorities**, against **the powers** of this dark world and against **the spiritual forces of evil** in the heavenly realms" (Ephesians 6:12).*

- **Rulers or "principalities"** *(Archas):* are the first ones, prominent ones

  References – Romans 8:38; 1 Corinthians 15:24; Ephesians 1:21, 3:10, 6:12; Colossians 1:16, 2:10; Titus 3:1

- **Authorities** – *(Exousia)* – the power of rule or government

Definition - Power exercised by rulers or other high position by virtue of office

Reference - 1 Corinthians 15:24; Ephesians 1:21, 2:2, 3:10, 6:12; Colossians 1:13, 1:16, 2:10, 2:15; Titus 3:1; 1 Peter 3:22

- **World forces of this darkness** – *(Kosmokrataras):* World rulers of darkness of this age

  Definition - Master spirits who are the world rulers of this present darkness

  Reference - Ephesians 6:12

- **Spiritual forces of wickedness in the heavenly places** *(Pneumatika poneria):* spiritual wickedness

  Definition - Spiritual forces that are wicked and inhabit the sphere above the earth

  Reference - Ephesians 6:12, 3:10

Here we will be looking at the fourth aspect of **spiritual forces of wickedness,** *(evil spirits or demons)*. In ministry, when we are ministering deliverance, these are the forces *(in most cases)*, which we're coming against.

An Organised System

When we are ministering, we have to recognise that there are other authorities, governments who are giving the orders to the front line demons *(or forces of wickedness)*. Satan has an organised system just like any army, including the army of God.

Let's take Moses who had millions of people to lead and exercise authority over, which he found impossible to cope with on his own, so he appointed wise and respectable men to have authority over thousands, hundreds and fifties and of tens, *(Deuteronomy 1:15)*. This is how we see the structure of the Church today with Jesus as the Head.

Satan however has a similar structure, although he can only be in one place at any one time, so obviously he has to delegate responsibility to other major spirits who can cover the nations. These authorities in turn give instructions to the spiritual forces of wickedness, who are sent to invade an individual's life.

> *Be alert and of sober mind. Your enemy the devil prowls around like a roaring lion looking for someone to devour.*
>
> *(1 Peter 5:8)*

Every man and woman has spiritual forces assigned to them that will come and torment them if they are given the opportunity. As I have already mentioned, one thing we can be thankful for is that Satan is not omnipresent, he can only be in one place at any one time, unlike God who *is* omnipresent – everywhere. God knows everything immediately, He knows our thoughts before we think them and our prayers before we pray them. Satan, on the other hand does not and cannot work like this.

Satan needs his spiritual forces to enforce his evil desires and to receive messages, as he needs to know whether his orders have been carried out successfully or not.

Evil Spirits or Demons

When Lucifer rebelled against God, he influenced other angels to join him. Just as he was cast down from heaven so too were they. Many bible teachers believe that a third of the angelic hosts were involved.

> *Then war broke out in heaven. Michael and his angels fought against the dragon, and the dragon and his angels fought back. But he was not strong enough, and they lost their place in heaven. The great dragon was hurled down – that ancient serpent called the devil, or Satan, who leads the whole world astray. He was hurled to the earth, and his angels with him.*
>
> *(Revelation 12:7-9)*

Are Evil Spirits fallen Angels?

Now it is said that these fallen angels are evil spirits. There is a big discrepancy here because scripture does not make it clear. In 2 Peter 2:4, it says that God put them into dungeons to be held for judgment. These are the fallen angels, not Satan. So the fallen angels are already bound!

In Jude 1:6 it also says,

> *And the angels who did not keep their positions of authority but abandoned their proper dwelling – these he has kept in darkness, bound with everlasting chains for judgment on the great Day.*

So if angels which were thrown out of heaven are bound, where do evil spirits come from?

Here are three suggestions as to where evil spirits could possibly come from:

Suggestion No 1.

Many bible scholars believe that millions of years may have elapsed between Genesis 1:1 and Genesis 1:2. They believe the spirits that are here on earth now were part of an original kingdom. Remember, God told Adam and Eve to be fruitful and multiply and replenish the earth. The word, *"replenish"* actually means, *"to fill up again with."*

The implication here is that the earth was full at some point before and had become empty or depleted and needed replenishing.

As we have already discovered, dinosaurs and other types of animals existed. Where did they come from? They are not talked about in the bible, but we know that they existed because there is proof *(archaeology, fossil finds and dinosaur bones etc.)* They did not come from our system, so it looks like there had to be a different kind of creation here, before Adam.

Suggestion No 2.

That evil spirits came from the unnatural offspring of angels and human women, prior to the flood in the days of Noah, *(Numbers 13:33; Genesis 6:4).* They were looked upon as giants, these offspring, and demi gods. They were very fearsome and evil and there is the possibility that when they died, their spirits which left their bodies are now wandering the earth!

Suggestion No 3.

That it was the time of the flood, when there was much wickedness and the Lord became grieved. He wiped mankind from the face of the earth and it is from those who died, whose spirits wander the earth *(1 Peter 3:19-20).* Then we see that Jesus during the three days of His death, *(before the resurrection),* went and preached to those who died in the flood.

So there are lots of question marks about the origin of evil spirits. You need to make up your own mind. One thing we can be sure of is that evil spirits and demons do exist. We may not know for sure where they come from, but we can be sure that they are real and that we have been given the means to be victorious over them.

What can Evil Spirits or Demons Do?

We know that **evil spirits are disembodied personalities,** actively opposing God's people and purposes serving, their master – Satan and harming people who bear the image of God. Their intent is to express their evil natures through people whom they have been holding captive. Their aim is to harm and ultimately cause the destruction of their victims.

So they can control – possess:

Let me just say something about possession, when someone says they are possessed, they probably are not. Many books speak about demons possessing people, but since 1984, when I began ministering in this area, I have only met one person who was.

It is rare for people to be totally possessed. I often talk about Satan possessing a certain part of the body, but it's not a **total possession.** Possession implies the total control of a person - his personality, mentally, physically and spiritually.

Evil spirits can:

Physically afflict   -   (Matthew 9:32; Mark 9:14-29)

Mentally deceive   -   (Genesis 3:1-5; Acts 5:3)
(they deceive through appealing to our carnal nature)

Emotionally disturb -   (2 Timothy 1:7)

Doctrinally delude   -   (1 Timothy 4:1; 1 John 4:1-2)

What are demons like?

They are intelligent   -   (Acts 16:16–18)

They are spirit   -   (Luke 10:17–20)

They are wicked   -   (Matthew 12:43–45)

They know their own end   - (Matthew 8:29; James 2:19)

Have supernatural strength - (Luke 8:29; Acts 19:11–17)

However they all have to bow their knee to the Name of Jesus Christ (Matthew 8:28–34; Mark 5:7; Luke 8:26–29).

Some Names of Demons

The bible shows us quite clearly in both the Old and New Testaments the sort of evil spirits of wickedness we are dealing with.

For instance in the Old Testament we see spirits of:

Treachery	-	(Judges 9:23)
Torment	-	(1 Samuel 16:14)
Prophesying spirits	-	(1 Samuel 18:10)
Spiritualism	-	(1 Samuel 28:8)
Lying spirits	-	(1 Kings 22:21)
Spirits leading to death	-	(2 Kings 19:7)
Dizziness	-	(Isaiah 19:14)
Spirits who destroy	-	(Jeremiah 51:1)
Prostitution	-	(Hosea 4:12)
Impurity	-	(Zechariah 13:2)

In the New Testament we see spirits of:

Dumbness	-	(Matthew 9:33)
Blindness & Dumbness	-	(Matthew 12:22)
Seizures *(epilepsy)*	-	(Matthew 17:18)
Spirit named Legion	-	(Luke 8:30)
Infirmity	-	(Luke 13:12)
Divination *(predicts future)*	-	(Acts 16:16)
Stupor	-	(Romans 11:8)
Deception	-	(1 Timothy 4:1-2)

❖

CHAPTER 6

Observations and Effects

The following pages consist of a simple graph, with references, activity, descriptions and how evil spirits were simply and effectively dealt with.

This is not meant to be a full account, but perhaps a beginning for further studies for yourself.

Demons – New Testament (Greek – Daimonion)

Reference	Activity/ Effect	Description	How dealt with	Notes/ Observations
Matthew 4:24	Recognised by people who brought them for deliverance	Demon possessed (demonized)	He healed them	- Deliverance comes within the general category of healing (many like this in a small area)
Matthew 8:16			Drove out the spirit with a word	
Matthew 9:33	Caused dumbness		Driven out	- Was able to speak again
Matthew 10:8			Drive out demons	- Deliverance was part of a wider commission the disciples had been given - It was a part of establishing God's kingdom on the earth - The disciple had received deliverance, "Freely you have received now freely give." We cannot minister in this way if we have not received ministry
Matthew 12:22	Caused blindness and dumbness	Demon possessed	Jesus healed him	- Deliverance is part of the healing ministry
Matthew 17:18	Seizures – throwing into fire and water		Rebuked the demon	- Deliverance is part of the healing ministry

Observations and Effects

Reference	Activity/ Effect	Description	How dealt with	Notes/ Observation
Mark 1:34	Were able to speak through person		Drove out many demons	- Jesus had AUTHORITY over demons and would not let them speak, why? Were all healed or delivered?
Mark 1:39			Drove out demons	- Preaching went with deliverance
Mark 3:15			Authority to drive out demons	- Authority was given by Jesus to the 12 disciples
Mark 7:25	Demon possession was recognised by parent, how is not stated	Possessed by an evil/ unclean spirit	Begged Jesus to drive the demon out of her daughter	- It was a child who was possessed - The child was under the parent's authority and this gave entry for Jesus' ministry - Willingness and seeking by parents for ministry
Mark 6:12-13			Drove out many demons	- Repentance was part of deliverance and healing
Mark 16:17			Will drive out demons	- These signs will accompany those who believe. Demons must be driven out in the Name of Jesus
Mark 16:9		Seven demons	Driven out	- Mary Magdalene was cleansed completely and went to serve Jesus in active ministry

Reference	Activity/ Effect	Description	How dealt with	Notes/ Observations
Luke 4:33	- Spoke through the man - Threw the man to the ground, violently	A demon, an evil/ unclean spirit	Jesus said "come out of him" Told demon to be quiet sternly	- Jesus exercised His authority in telling the demon to be quiet - Demon referred to itself/themselves as US!
Luke 8:29	- Lived alone without clothes in a solitary place - Gave supernatural – extra strength	Evil/ unclean spirit; Demon possessed	Commanded it to come out	- Jesus' authority was recognised and truth about Him spoken - Afterwards he was dressed and in his right mind (Mark 5:15). Implications for psychiatrically ill - Many demons in one man, Jesus asked their names
Luke 9:42	- Boy was thrown to the ground as he neared Jesus - Convulsions, screaming and foaming at the mouth (Mark 9:20)	Demon, evil/ unclean spirit	Rebuked	- Lack of faith highlighted - Again parental authority over child and seeking ministry gave Jesus entry into boy's life
Luke 10:17			Submitted to the Name of Jesus	- Was not confined to the twelve apostles

Observations and Effects

Reference	Activity/ Effect	Description	How dealt with	Notes/ Observations
Luke 11:14	Muteness		Driven out by the finger of God (v20)	- Driving out demons was described by Jesus as coming of kingdom amongst them - Jesus had words of knowledge (v17) - Spirits can return with others if person is not filled with the Holy Spirit - Demons can occupy different parts of person (mind, body, etc.), (v22 divides up the spoil)
Acts 8:7	Came out with shrieks		Came out	
Acts 16:16	Enabled the girl to predict the future	A spirit by which she predicted the future	"In the Name of Jesus I command you to come out of her"	- Authority in the Name of Jesus was used
Acts 19:12		Evil spirits	Left them	- Paul continued with the instructions given to disciples - The demons recognised the authority of Jesus and Paul, but not those using his name

Reference	Activity/ Effect	Description	How dealt with	Notes/ Observations
Romans 8:38		Demons		- Demons and angles are distinguished (demons are also described as heavenly rulers – NIV)
Romans 11:8	Stupor	A spirit	Given by God	- Given by God so they could see or hear spiritually
1 Corinthians 10:19-22		Idols/ demons		- Sacrifices offered to idols are offered to demons (Deuteronomy 32:17) - Implications for world religions
1 Corinthians 12:10		Spirits		- Need ability to distinguish between spirits, suggests different types of spirits
1 Timothy 4:1-2	Deception	Deceiving spirits		- Demons can teach through people – "hypocritical liars" - Are demons and deceiving spirits the same? - Leads to people losing their faith and turning to legalism - People can appear to be spiritual and teaching the truth

Observations and Effects

Reference	Activity/ Effect	Description	How dealt with	Notes/ Observations
James 2:19		Demons		- Demons know of God and are fearful of Him - Recognise the authority of God in believers and are fearful, as they have to submit
1 Peter 3:19		Spirits		- Are these the spirits of people who were preached to, or spirits from sons of God (Genesis) and women who came together? - Why were they preached to?
1 John 4:1			Tested	- Spirits can communicate through people and not always recognisable
1 John 4:3	Spirits of Antichrist			- Need to be "tested," through "Word of God" and discerned - Spirits not acknowledging Jesus as Lord are under authority of "spirit of antichrist"
1 John 4:6	Spirit of falsehood			- Is in the world

Reference	Activity/ Effect	Description	How dealt with	Notes/ Observations
Revelation 16:13	Perform miraculous signs, influence kings of the world and draw them to battle	Evil spirits, looked like frogs, Spirits of demons		- Came out of the mouth of the dragon and false prophet
Revelation 18:2		Demons		- Demons can have homes and haunts, (City of Babylon is mentioned)
		Evil spirits		- Associated with adultery and excessive luxury

Evil Spirits – Old Testament (Hebrew – Ruach)

Reference	Activity/ Effect	Description	How to deal with	Notes/Observations
Judges 9:23	Treachery/ revolt	Evil spirit		- God sent an evil spirit to divide a people against their ruler. His judgement on previous sin
1 Samuel 16:14	Tormentor	Evil spirit	Music played to him	- Evil spirit was sent by God after God's spirit had departed - Saul recognised (along with others) that it was an evil spirit troubling him - Evil spirit came and went
1 Samuel 18:10	Anger/ murder	Evil spirit		- Came forcefully on Saul
1 Samuel 19:9				- As above

Observations and Effects

Reference	Activity/ Effect	Description	How dealt with	Notes/ Observation
1 Samuel 28:8		Spirit of Samuel (not ruach)		- Called by spiritualist/ medium, prophecy
1 Kings 22:22 2 Chronicles 18:20	Lying	A spirit		- A spirit came before the Lord with suggestion - The Lord sent the spirit
1 Kings 22:22	Lead a person to his death	A spirit		- Spirit put lies in the mouth of the prophets - The Lord put the spirits into the person
Isaiah 19:14	Dizziness	A spirit (not ruach)		
Isaiah 37:7	Directs the action	A spirit (not ruach)		- Sent by God to direct king's actions
Jeremiah 5:17	Destruction	A spirit		- Sent by God in judgment
Hosea 4:12	- Prostitution - Leads them astray	A spirit		
Zechariah 13:2	Impurity	A spirit		- Removed by the Lord from the land

Devil (Accuser) – New Testament (Greek – Diabolos)

Reference	Activity/ Effect	Description	How dealt with	Notes/ Observations
Matthew 4:1	- Temptation to exercise self and power against the Father's will - Scripture twisted to deceive	The tempter The devil Satan	Truth of scripture spoken out	- Satan is king of this world, went to Jesus King of heavenly realm. Humans get tempted by lesser spirits - We need to know who we are dealing with (as Jesus knew who He was dealing with) - Tempted when alone – need fellowship - In ministry we must only do what we see the Father doing (John 5:19)
Matthew 13:38-39	Sons of the evil one	Enemy The devil The evil one	At the end of the age angels will throw sons of the evil one into the fiery furnace	
Matthew 25:41		The devil and his angels		- Devil has angels under his command/ authority - Are demons fallen angels?
Luke 8:12	Takes away God's Word	The devil		- In evangelism we are involved in warfare against the devil. Prayer should reflect this

Observations and Effects

Reference	Activity/ Effect	Description	How dealt with	Notes/ Observations
John 6:70	Betrayer	A devil		- Doing what the devil wanted him to do - Tried to destroy what God was doing - God turned this to His ultimate end
John 8:44	Deception	- Liar - Father of Lies - Murderer - A father	Speaks truth to the Pharisees	- If we are not of Jesus we are subject to Satan's kingdom - Jews, in not accepting Jesus belonged to the devil who was described as their father - They were not aware of the devil's activity in their lives
John 13:2	Betrayal	The devil		- Our actions can be influenced by the devil and we can be aware of it
Acts 13:8-10 (John 8:44)	- Enemy of righteous - Deceit - Trickery	Child of the devil	Paul caused sorcerer to go blind for a short while	- Signs and wonders led to conversions of the Proconsul
Ephesians 4:27		The devil	Living righteously	- Devil can get a foothold in Christian's life through anger, idleness, lying

Reference	Activity/ Effect	Description	How dealt with	Notes/ Observations
Ephesians 6:11	Schemes – injure or kill Christians	The devil	Putting on the whole amour of God	- Devil plans and makes strategies against church and Christians - We are fighting against rulers, authorities, powers (of this world), spiritual forces of evil (in the heavenly realms) - Suggests hierarchy and authority and that we are not contending directly with Satan
Ephesians 6:12				- Christians need to be properly equipped to do battle: truth, righteousness, faith, proclamation, salvation, Word of God, prayer in the Spirit with all kinds of prayers
1 Timothy 3:6	Trap	The devil	Judgement	- Devil will be judged. The devil sets traps for people to deceive, entice and lie
2 Timothy 2:26	- Takes captive - Traps	The devil	Repentance	- People are ensnared by the devil to do his will

Observations and Effects

Reference	Activity/ Effect	Description	How dealt with	Notes/ Observations
Hebrews 2:14	- Held the power of death	The devil		- Through His death, Jesus destroys the devil and frees people from fear of death which enslaves
James 4:7	- Quarrelling, fighting adultery, coveting, division	The devil	Submission to God	- By resisting devil in thinking, action, word, prayer, praise - he will flee
1 Peter 5:8	Devourer	Enemy	- Self control - Alert - Resistance - Standing firm in faith - Humility - Prayer	- Again suggests we are involved in a battle and that we need weapons - Can consume people, totally occupying a person's thoughts and actions
1 John 3:8	Sin	The devil	By Jesus	- Jesus destroys the damage done to a person by sin, which opens up the way for the devil to enter a person's life - "Children of the devil" applies to any person who is sinning

Reference	Activity/ Effect	Description	How dealt with	Notes/ Observations
Jude 9		The devil	The Lord rebuke you	- Archangel Michael argued with the devil – conflict - Would not slander him, but used authority of the Lord to rebuke him - This suggests we should address demons and the devil
Revelation 2:10	Put some of us in prison	The devil		- Can control world events and bring persecution to Christians
Revelation 12:7-9	Leads the whole world astray	The devil The great dragon Ancient serpent	Battle with angels	- Michael (archangel) and the angels (hierarchy) battle against the devil and win - Is this a future event (Jude 6) or has it happened - Can the devil and his angels still enter God's presence
Revelation 20:1-3	Deceiver of the nations	The dragon Ancient serpent The devil Satan	By an angel from heaven, who seized him and locked him in the abyss	- Main function of the devil is to deceive nations - Angels from heaven had power over Satan (comes with God's authority)

Satan's Hierarchy - Old and New Testament

Reference	Activity/ Effect	Description	How dealt with	Notes/ Observations
Leviticus 17:7		DEMONS Goat idols/ demons		- Animal idols were representatives of demons - Implications for world religions, animism and demonic activity is released in this
Deuteronomy 32:17		Demons, which are not God (shad)		- Sacrifices can be made to demons – idol worship (see above)
Psalm 106:37		Demons (shad)		- Sons and daughters were sacrificed to demons, people thought they were gods
Romans 8:38		Demons (heavenly rulers)		- Angels seem to be differentiated here from demons
Luke 11:15 also Mark 3:23		BEELZEBUB /PRINCE Prince of demons		
Daniel 10:13	Prince of the Persian kingdom	Prince of a country	By an archangel from God	- Michael, one of the chief princes, was released by God through Daniel's prayer and battled for 21 days
John 12:31 14:30 16:11		Prince of this world – Satan		- Devil described as "prince over the earth" - Probably chief prince like Michael

Reference	Activity/ Effect	Description	How dealt with	Notes/ Observations
Luke 11:26		More wicked spirits		- Says that some evil spirits are more wicked than others
Luke 10:19			Authority from Jesus	- To overcome <u>all</u> the power of the enemy - Different manifestations
Romans 8:38		Angels, demons/ heavenly rulers, powers		- All differentiated
Ephesians 6:12		Devil, rulers, authorities, spiritual forces of evil		- All differentiated
Ephesians 6:12	<u>RULERS -KOSMEKRATOR (Greek)</u>			

❖

PART TWO

Healing God's Provision for You

❖

CHAPTER 7

Healing is for You

God's will is to heal. It is important to remember that in any given situation, we should always look into the Word of God for the truth. The Church of today has so many ideas where ministry is concerned – they seem to have their own doctrines – especially in the area of setting their captives free.

So let's go back to scripture:

We realise that healing and deliverance quite often go together – deliverance in the majority of cases, will itself bring about the healing of the individual. In fact someone once said, *"Salvation will bring complete deliverance and healing."* One thing that we know is that Christians do get sick at times, for a variety of reasons.

As we go on in our study of scripture we will discover that sickness is not the will of God so therefore must be the will of Satan.

Jesus knew that sickness was caused by demonic influence or bondage. In such cases healing had to include the expulsion of the demonic influence which was causing the disease or manifestation of sickness.

In the four Gospels we find twenty-eight recorded incidents of deliverance compared with fifty-two healings. In the book of Acts there are a further ten incidents of deliverance compared with the eleven reports of healing. In the instance of deliverance, like those who needed healing, some concerned only a single person but some are multiple events involving many people.

God's will is to Heal

Before we go any further we need to establish whether it is God's will to heal.

Proverbs 4:20-22 (KJV) says,

*My son, attend to my words; incline thine ear unto my sayings. Let them not depart from thine eyes; keep them in the midst of thine heart. For they are life unto those that find them, and **health to all their flesh.***

Christians accept that God is **able** to heal, but they find it difficult to accept God's **willingness** and **desire** to heal them personally.

Not knowing His will causes us to doubt and where there is doubt there is no faith and without faith it is impossible to receive from God.

God's will concerning healing is firstly revealed in His name, Jehovah Rapha – the God who heals.

<u>Rapha</u>: to mend, to sew, to cure, to heal, to repair, to thoroughly make whole.

If thou wilt diligently hearken to the voice of the Lord thy God, and wilt do that which is right in his sight, and wilt give ear to his commandments, and keep all his statutes, I will put none of these diseases upon thee, which I have brought upon the Egyptians: **for I am the Lord that healeth thee.**

(Exodus 15:26 KJV)

Attend to My Words

This is God's recipe for life and health but notice it reads, "Attend to MY WORDS." What words? We need a firm foundation of scripture to understand what God's Words are to us. His truth sets us free *(John 8:32)*. It is only then that we will be able to stand, in the situations and circumstances that come our way. **We need the written Word so that Jesus can become the Living Word within our lives today.**

We need to continually confess, "God is my healer." The more you say it, the more you will believe it and you will turn to Him first before any kind of method or medication.

David was a man who knew God in a personal way. He knew Him as the God who healed him.

O Lord my God, I cried unto thee, and thou hast healed me.

(Psalm 30:2 KJV)

Many are the afflictions of the righteous: but the Lord delivereth him out of them all. He keepeth all his bones: not one of them is broken.

(Psalm 34:19-20 KJV)

God is revealing Himself through all these verses as a God who will restore health and heal wounds.

In Malachi 3:6 (KJV) it says,

For I am the Lord, I change not…

We know that Jesus is referred to as being the Word:

In the beginning was the Word, and the Word was with God, and the Word was God. He was in the beginning with God. All things were made through Him, and without Him nothing was made that was made.

(John 1:1-3 NKJV)

In Him was life and light:

In him was life, and the life was the light of men. And the light shines in the darkness, and the darkness did not comprehend it. There was a man sent out from God, whose name was John. This man came for a witness, to bear witness of the Light, that all through him might believe. He was not that light, but was sent to bear witness of that Light.

(John 1:4-8 NKJV)

Yet all who did receive him, to those who believed in his name, he gave the right to become children of God... The word became flesh and made his dwelling among us. We have seen the glory, the glory of the One and Only, who came from the father, full of grace and truth.

(John 1:12, 14 NKJV)

But Jesus is also referred to as the Sacrificial Lamb, *"For Christ, our Passover lamb, has been sacrificed"* (1 Corinthians 5:7). A voice in the wilderness cried out,

Behold the Lamb of God, which taketh away the sin of the world.

(John 1:29 KJV)

When Jesus came He started where God's voice left off in the past. He called everybody, the sinful, the sick, the fearful and the faithless to come to Him. Those who sat in the shadow of death lifted up their heads and listened.

John the Baptist sent messengers to find out about Jesus:

And when John had heard in prison about the works of Christ, he sent two of his disciples and said to Him, "Are you the Coming One, or do we look for another?" Jesus answered and said to them, "Go and tell John the things which you hear and see: The blind receive their sight and the lame walk; the lepers are cleansed and the deaf hear; the dead are raised up and the poor have the gospel preached to them.

(Matthew 11:2-5 NKJV)

God was calling them. The poor heard the good news. Those enslaved by the devil were released. The blind received their sight. The oppressed were liberated. The broken-hearted realised that God loved them. The Unique One had come. He came not only with a message but with a ministry.

But now He has obtained a more excellent ministry, inasmuch as He is also Mediator of a better covenant, which was established on better promises.

(Hebrews 8:6 NKJV)

He expressed it in word and in deed. He had come to establish a New Covenant. The gradual revelation of God's plan of redemption was coming into full view. All the altars, ceremonies and covenants were to find their complete meaning in the New Covenant, established by Jesus.

❖

CHAPTER 8

The Passover

At the last supper with His disciples Jesus celebrated the Passover. They remembered their deliverance, which their fathers had obtained by the blood of the lambs. Although the disciples may not have understood the meaning of His words, they were asked to take His body and blood through the bread and the wine as a New Covenant for the forgiveness of sin.

"They were not required to understand but to trust the Saviour, as man was asked in the beginning to trust his Creator. They were looking at the lamb. He was about to go to His altar, Calvary."[1]

To understand fully the implications of what happened at the second Passover *(Calvary)* we need to turn back the pages of scripture to the first Passover, which we find in Exodus 12:1-6, 11-13.

And if the household is too small for the lamb, let him and his neighbour next to his house take it according to the number of persons; according to each man's need you shall make your count for the lamb. Your lamb shall be without blemish, a male, of the first year. You may take it from the sheep or from the goats. Now you shall keep it until the fourteenth day of the same month. Then the whole assembly of the congregation of Israel shall kill it at twilight.

(Exodus 12:4-6 NKJV)

This is how you are to eat it; with your cloak tucked into your belt, your sandals on your feet, and your staff in your hand. Eat it in haste; it is the Lord's Passover. On that same night I will pass through Egypt and strike down every first born – both men and animals – and I will bring judgement on all the gods of Egypt. I am the Lord. The blood will be a sign for you on the houses where you are; and when I see the blood, I will pass over you. No destructive plague will touch you when I strike Egypt.

(Exodus 12:11-13 NKJV)

Notice in the third verse it says, "*Tell the whole community of Israel that each man has to take a lamb for his family and his household.*" That word, "whole community" implies that God wants to reach all. For scripture tells us that Jesus was the reconciliation of the whole world *(Romans 11:15)* – every single person – man, woman and child.

This Passover was God's protection and provision for His people. The blood that was sprinkled upon the door posts was for protection, a sign for deliverance, not only from death, but also from the slavery in Egypt.

One thing we can be sure of as Christians is that we are in the world but not of it *(2 Corinthians 10:3)*. We have been set free from being enslaved to the world, through the overcoming Christ:

> *For if we have been united together in the likeness of His death, certainly we also shall be in the likeness of His resurrection, knowing this, that our old man was crucified with Him, that the body of sin might be done away with, that we should no longer be slaves of sin.*
> *(Romans 6:5-6 NKJV)*

> *But Christ came as High Priest of the good things to come, with the greater and more perfect tabernacle not made with hands, that is, not of this creation. Not with the blood of goats and calves, but with His own blood He entered the Most Holy Place once for all, having obtained eternal redemption.*

> *For if the blood of bulls and goats and the ashes of a heifer, sprinkling the unclean, sanctifies for the purifying of the flesh, how much more shall the blood of Christ, who through the eternal Spirit offered Himself without spot to God, cleanse your conscience from dead works to serve the living God?*

> *And for this reason He is the Mediator of the new covenant, by means of death, for the redemption of the transgressions*

under the first covenant, that those who are called may receive the promise of the eternal inheritance.

(Hebrews 9:11-15 NKJV)

We can I believe, remain free from the sicknesses and diseases that so often afflict. For when Satan sees the Blood of Christ, there is no way that he is able to afflict, for the scripture says no destructive plague will touch you.

Because you have made the Lord, who is my refuge, even the Most High, your habitation, no evil shall befall you, nor shall any plague came near your dwelling; for He shall give His angels charge over you, to keep you in all your ways.

(Psalm 91:9-11 NKJV)

Stripped of his Powers

Jesus stripped the enemy and having disarmed the powers and authorities, He made a public spectacle of them, triumphing over them by the Cross *(Colossians 2:15)*. For this reason we know that Christ became the New Covenant that we might receive an eternal inheritance *(Hebrews 9:15)*. He was the only ransom which could be given to set us free.

For when Christ came into the world He said,

Sacrifice and offering You did not desire, but a body You have prepared for Me. In burnt offerings and sacrifices for sin You had no pleasure. Then I said, "Behold, I have come – In the volume of the book it is written of Me – To do Your will, O God."

(Hebrews 10:5-7 NKJV)

By one sacrifice He has made perfect forever those who are being made holy.

But this Man, after He had offered one sacrifice for sins forever, sat down at the right hand of God, from that time waiting till His enemies are made His footstool. For by one offering He has perfected forever those who are being sanctified.

But the Holy Spirit also witnesses to us; for after He had said before, "This is the covenant that I will make with them after those days, says the Lord: I will put My laws into their hearts, and in their minds I will write them," then He adds, "Their sins and their lawless deeds I will remember no more."

(Hebrews 10:12-17 NKJV)

We read earlier in Exodus 12:1-13 that God's first provision of healing and health was in the lamb that was without defect. Jesus became the second and final perfect Sacrificial Lamb, which we are told to take of and eat.

The Bread of Life

Scripture also refers to Jesus as the Bread of Life, for Jesus said, *"Do not work for food that spoils, but for food that endures to eternal life, which the Son of Man will give you"* (*John 6:27*). On Him God the Father has placed a seal of approval. For the Bread of God is He who comes down from heaven and gives life to the world.

The disciples said to Jesus,

"Sir," they said, "from now on give us this bread." Then Jesus declared, "I am the bread of life, He who comes to

me will never go hungry, and he who believes in me will never be thirsty."

(John 6:34-35)

I am the living bread that came down from heaven. If anyone eats of this bread, he will live forever. This bread is my flesh, which I will give for the life of the world.

(John 6:50-51)

Healing then I believe, is for us and our families. As we feed on the Lamb *(the Rhema Word of God)*, then no plague will come near our dwelling and sickness has no right to come into our households *(Exodus 12:23)*.

Sickness is an intruder.

❖

CHAPTER 9

Definite Fulfilment

A great part of the ministry of Jesus Christ was the healing of the sick. We see in Matthew 8:17 that this was a definite fulfilment of what was spoken through the prophet Isaiah.

Surely He has borne our griefs and carried our sorrows; yet we esteemed Him stricken, smitten by God, and afflicted. But He was wounded for our transgressions, He was bruised for our iniquities; the chastisement for our peace was upon Him, and by His stripes we are healed.

All we like sheep have gone astray; we have turned, every one, to his own way; and the Lord has laid on Him the iniquity of us all. He was oppressed and He was afflicted, yet He opened not His mouth; He was led as a lamb to the slaughter, and as a sheep before its shearers is silent, so He opened not His mouth.

(Isaiah 53:4-7 KJV)

Jesus it would seem, has already taken our infirmities, and bore our sicknesses *(v4)*. In 1 Peter 2:24 we find the words, *"He himself bore our sins in his body on the tree, so that we might die to sins and live for righteousness; by his wounds YOU HAVE BEEN HEALED."*

Again in Psalm 103:3 (NKJV) the first two benefits mentioned are:

- Who forgives all your iniquities
- Who heals all your diseases

Sicknesses on the Cross

There are therefore, in clear words of scripture, grounds for believing that sicknesses was dealt with at Calvary. In Matthew it describes several incidents of physical healing from the ministry of Jesus.

When evening came, many who were demon-possessed were brought to him, and he drove out the spirits with a word and healed all the sick.

(Matthew 8:16)

The above scripture mentions demon-possession and sickness, so in these circumstances what did Jesus do? He drove the demons out and healed the sick irrespective of the sick person's particular condition. Matthew continues to say *(v17)* that this was to fulfil what was spoken through the prophet Isaiah.

Can we take this to mean that God's plan for each one of us is that we can be and should be free from sin and sickness? I believe it does. We know that what Jesus did during His early ministry is now available for all of us, through the Cross.

Jesus never sinned, yet He bore our sins in His body.

> *For to this you were called, because Christ also suffered for us, leaving us an example, that you should follow His steps: "Who committed no sin, Nor was deceit found in His mouth;" who, when He was reviled, did not revile in return; when He suffered, He did not threaten, but committed Himself to Him who judges righteously; who Himself bore our sins in His own body on the tree, that we, having died to sins, might live for righteousness – by whose stripes you were healed.*
>
> *(1 Peter 2:21-24 NKJV)*

A Total Work

He was never sick as far as we know, yet carried our sickness on the cross. He also took our grief and sorrow, the whole sorrowful mess of humanity. What God did for us in the death of Christ, was a total work of healing and deliverance.

> *I will deliver you from the Jewish people, as well as from the Gentiles, to whom I now sent you, to open their eyes, in order to turn them from darkness to light, and from the*

power of Satan to God, that they may receive forgiveness of sins and an inheritance among those who are sanctified by faith in Me.

(Acts 26:17-18 NKJV)

Through this deliverance we are able to receive forgiveness and be reconciled to God, and to enjoy a loving relationship with Him.

Principles and Patterns

The ministry of Jesus began only after His baptism and anointing by the Holy Spirit.

When all the people were being baptised, Jesus was baptised too. And as he was praying, heaven was open and the Holy Spirit descended on him in bodily form like a dove. And a voice came from heaven: "You are my Son, whom I love; with you I am well pleased." Now Jesus himself was about thirty years old when he began his ministry.

(Luke 3:21-23)

After His baptism, Jesus began an active ministry. He delivered all who came to Him from every kind of sickness.

In His ministry Jesus:

- Preached the Word
- Healed the sick
- Cast out demons
- Raised the dead

Preached the Word:

And again he entered into Capernaum after some days; and it was noised that he was in the house. And straightway many were gathered together, insomuch that there was no room to receive them, no, not so much as about the door: and he preached the word unto them.

(Mark 2:1-2 KJV)

Healed the sick:

And again, departing from the region of Tyre and Sidon, He came through the midst of the region of Decapolis to the Sea of Galilee. Then they brought to Him one who was deaf and had an impediment in his speech, and they begged Him to put His hand on him. And He took him aside from the multitude, and put His fingers in his ears, and He spat and touched his tongue. Then looking up to heaven, He said to him "Ephphatha," that is, "Be opened."

Immediately his ears were opened, and the impediment of his tongue was loosed, and he spoke plainly. Then He commanded them that they should tell no one; but the more He commanded them, the more widely they proclaimed it. And they were astonished beyond measure, saying "He has done all things well. He makes both the deaf to hear and the mute to speak."

(Mark 7:31-37 NKJV)

Cast out demons:

And when they had come to the multitude, a man came to Him, kneeling down to him and saying, "Lord, have mercy on my son, for he is an epileptic and suffers severely; for he often falls into the fire and often into the water. So I brought him to Your disciples, but they could not cure him."

Then Jesus answered and said, "O faithless and perverse generation, how long shall I be with you? How long shall I bear with you? Bring him here to Me." And Jesus rebuked the demon, and he came out of him; and the child was cured from that very hour.

(Matthew 17:14-18 NKJV)

Raised from the dead:

Then Jesus, again groaning in Himself, came to the tomb. It was a cave, and a stone lay against it. Jesus said, "Take away the stone." Martha, the sister of him who was dead, said to Him, "Lord, by this time there is a stench, for he has been dead four days." Jesus said to her, "Did I not say to you that if you would believe you would see the glory of God?"

Then they took away the stone from the place where the dead man was lying. And Jesus lifted up His eyes and said, "Father, I thank You that You heard Me. And I know that You always hear Me, but because of the people who are standing by I said this, that they may believe that You sent Me." Now when He said these things, He cried with a loud voice, "Lazarus, come forth!" And he who had died came out bound hand and foot with graveclothes, and his face was wrapped with a cloth. Jesus said to them, "Loose him, and let him go."

(John 11:38-44 NKJV)

The gospels frequently state that Jesus' healing works were motivated by love and compassion and sometimes pity, for the sick.

When he saw the crowds, he had compassion on them, because they were harassed and helpless, like sheep without a shepherd.

(Matthew 9:36)

In Matthew 14:14, we see once again that Jesus had compassion on the people and healed the sick.

The Presence of Faith

By this time in His ministry people were flocking to hear this man, for they were amazed at His teaching. For whatever reason they came, Jesus saw them through the eyes of a shepherd who had compassion for His sheep. Later on in the same chapter we see that Jesus did not only heal the sick but also fed them, bringing complete satisfaction to their spiritual and physical needs.

It is amazing to me that Jesus was more able to heal the sick in the presence of faith, which puts the responsibility upon us as individuals. This means that we must be willing to respond because we have heard the good news and to activate our will, reaching out in faith to receive. It is only then that Jesus can restore and heal us.

We see five very important steps to clarify this statement in Mark 5:25-31, where the woman who was subjected to bleeding for twelve years, came to the end of her own resources.

Step one:

> *For she had suffered a great deal under the care of many doctors and had spent all she had, yet instead of getting better she grew worse.*
>
> *(Mark 5:26)*

If we are honest with ourselves, often this is the very place we come to, before we can receive.

With the National Health system and many kinds of other private clinics in place, it is easy to turn to these resources in order to seek physical and emotional healing. Although I believe these systems should be in place, it should not lead to our bankruptcy and poverty. In other words if we rely solely on the world's system, God is not able to fulfil His provision and bring wholeness to our lives.

Don't Rely on another Practitioner

We see a good example of this in 2 Chronicles 16:7-14. Because Asa the king of Judah relied on another king and not upon the Lord his God, his enemy escaped him. Yet when he upon relied on the Lord, they were delivered into his hands.

> *For the eyes of the Lord range throughout the earth to strengthen those hearts which are fully committed to him.*
>
> *(2 Chronicles 16:9)*

For when we look to man, God tells us that this is a foolish thing. The result of this can only bring affliction, in Asa's case, a disease in his feet *(v12)*. Though this disease was severe, he still did not seek help from the Lord, only from physicians.

Step two:

When she heard about Jesus, she came up behind Him [in faith] in the crowd and touched his cloak...
(Mark 5:27 emphasis added)

Why? Because she had heard the Good News that this man who had come, was healing the sick. She simply believed the message, a revelation that she was determined to follow. What had she to lose, after all, she had lost everything already.

Step three:

She had created a faith image of Jesus, for she thought, *"If I just touch his clothes, I will be healed" (Mark 5:28).* There was no doubt in her heart or mind.

Step four:

She pushed through the crowd seeking just to touch His garment, which could not have been an easy task in itself.

Immediately her bleeding stopped and she felt in her body that she was freed from her suffering.
(Mark 5:29)

She must have been frail, weak maybe, even feeling bullied perhaps, as the crowd was pushing and shoving against each other to see Jesus. But she thought of nothing other than how to achieve her goal and as she touched His garment, she received her reward, the healing she so desired.

Step five:

At once Jesus realized that power had gone out from him. He turned around in the crowd and asked, "Who touched

my clothes?" "You see the people crowding against you,"
his disciples answered, "and yet you can ask, 'Who
touched me?'"

(Mark 5:30-31)

There are many of us who are inquisitive, wanting to go along with the crowd, but not receiving anything. We will even come into the presence of God to fellowship but receive nothing, because we do not come in faith to receive!

In Mathew 8:5-13 we read the account of Jesus and the Centurion. Jesus was especially moved by this man's great faith:

Now when Jesus had entered Capernaum, a centurion
came to Him, pleading with Him, saying, "Lord, my
servant is lying at home paralysed, dreadfully tormented."
And Jesus said to him, "I will came and heal him."

The centurion answered and said, "Lord, I am not worthy
that You should come under my roof. But only speak a
word, and my servant will be healed. For I also am a man
under authority, having soldiers under me. And I say to
this one, 'Go,' and he goes; and to another, 'Come,' and he
comes; and to my servant, 'Do this,' and he does it."

When Jesus heard it, He marveled, and said to those who
followed, "Assuredly, I say to you, I have not found such
great faith, not even in Israel...

Then Jesus said to the centurion, "Go your way; and
as you have believed, so let it be done for you." And his
servant was healed that same hour.

(Matthew 8:5-10, 13 NKJV)

Jesus also observed supernaturally the faith and determination of the "bed carriers" as they carried the cripple.

Since they could not get him to Jesus because of the crowd, they made an opening in the roof above Jesus by digging through it and then lowered the mat the man was lying on.

(Mark 2:4)

What lengths these men were prepared to go to for their brother! Their persistence was extreme yet fruitful. Maybe we have made our Christianity too polite or even too "English?"

Jesus never at any time turned anyone away, but healed all those who came to Him. Although at times, He was apparently aware that the Spirit was especially ready to move in power.

...and the power of the Lord was present to heal them.
(Luke 5:17 KJV)

No Performance

Frequently the Lord would heal many, one after another, in large meetings or gatherings, which we can call Holy Spirit mass crusades! *(Matthew 4:23-25, 14:14, 15:30)*. Jesus would not do miracles for those who only wanted to test Him or be entertained, such as the Scribes and Pharisees as described in Matthew:

Then some of the scribes and Pharisees answered, saying, "Teacher, we want to see a sign from You." But He answered and said to them, "An evil and adulterous generation seeks after a sign, and no sign will be given to it except the sign of the prophet Jonah. For as Jonah was three days and three nights in the belly of the great fish, so will the Son of Man be three days and three nights in the heart of the earth.

(Matthew 12:38-40 NKJV)

Jesus was in no way going to perform for any man, whether Pharisees or teachers, even if they had authority as leaders. He had not come into this world only as a prophet, to fulfil what the prophets foretold. Jonah went through the trauma of being imprisoned by a huge fish for three days and three nights to indicate and point the way to the death and resurrection of Christ.

Jesus' Calling Card

This then was the purpose and destiny for which Jesus had been predestined. The salvation of man. Jesus had not come to perform signs and wonders – these were just His calling card – proof that the kingdom of God had come. For the miracles that Jesus performed such as the casting out of demons, healing the sick and power over nature, were the indication and proof that Satan's power on this earth had been broken. Therefore *"The time has come,"* He said, *"The kingdom of God is near"* (Mark 1:15).

Jesus' miracles also have another purpose, to show us what the kingdom of God is like and to reveal a glimpse of God's love, peace and joy to those that He has predestined to be adopted as His sons.

Just as He chose us in Him before the foundation of the world, that we should be holy and without blame before Him in love, having predestined us to adoption as sons by Jesus Christ to Himself, according to the good pleasure of His will...

(Ephesians 1:4-5 NKJV)

Resistance from the Pharisees to this kingdom ministry deeply grieved the Lord. An illustration of this is seen in Mark 3:1-6. Here we see Jesus in a synagogue on a Sabbath day and a man with a shrivelled hand was there. The Pharisees were watching to see if Jesus would heal on the Sabbath, but the heart of Jesus was only for the man. Then He said to the man who had the withered hand,

"Step forward." Then He said to them, "Is it lawful on the Sabbath to do good or to do evil, to save life or to kill?" But they kept silent. And when He had looked around at them with anger, being grieved by the hardness of their hearts, He said to the man, "Stretch out your hand." And he stretched it out, and his hand was restored as whole as the other.

(Mark 3:3-5 NKJV)

This is one of the few times we see that Jesus was angry for the lack of compassion that these religious leaders had. Jesus was not healing the sick on the Sabbath to be awkward, but because He was opposed to anything which bound or enslaved people. He recognised that the forces of darkness were connected with man's physical infirmities. In opposing these infirmities, He was showing His opposition to Satan and his kingdom.

Patterns and Methods

Jesus used many patterns and methods during His healing ministry.

- **Sometimes it was a touch,** as with Peter's mother-in-law, *(Matthew 8:15)*. She was laying in bed with a fever when Jesus simply touched her hand and the fever left her and she got up and began to wait on them.

- **Other times it was a prayer** to the Father and then a command, as in John 11:41-44,

    So they took away the stone. Then Jesus looked up and said, "Father, I thank you that you have heard me..." When he had said this, Jesus called in a loud voice "Lazarus, come out!" The dead man came out...
    (John 11:41, 43-44)

- Jesus would often speak this way – **a word of command** was often on His lips – a word like, **"Go,"** to the Centurion in Matthew 8:5-13.

- **"Rise,"** to the paralytic in Luke 5:17-26. **"Stretch out,"** to the man with a withered hand in Luke 6:6-10.

- And **"Arise,"** to the son of the widow in Nain, in Luke 7:11-17.

- On other occasions Jesus used **spittle to make mud** for the blind man's eyes *(John 9:6-7)*, then with **a command** *"Go and wash your face in the pool of Siloam."*

In obedience and faith he went and washed, then went home, seeing.

- Mark 7:33 speaks of when **Jesus spat and touched the man's tongue.** This would seem strange to us if we sensed the Lord telling us to carry out such an act.

- The command on this occasion was, **"Be Opened!"** then the man's tongue was loosed and he began to speak plainly.

- Sometimes Jesus had to pray more than once for the needy person to be healed, as in the case of the blind man of Bethsaida *(Mark 8:22-26)*. When Jesus spat on the man's eyes He said:

"Do you see anything?" He looked up and said, "I see people; they look like trees walking around."
(Mark 8:23-24)

So Jesus in response prayed once more, it was only then that the man received complete healing, his sight had been restored, seeing everything clearly.

Most of the time, Jesus healed within the public view, though occasionally He would withdraw, especially from a negative environment, healing privately as in the case of Jairus' daughter.

When He came in, He said to them, "Why make this commotion and weep? The child is not dead, but sleeping." And they laughed Him to scorn. But when He had put them all out, He took the father and the mother of the child, and those who were with Him, and entered where the child was lying. Then He took the child by the hand, and said to her, "Talitha, cumi," which is translated, "Little girl, I say to you, arise." Immediately the girl arose and walked, for she was twelve years of age. And they were overcome with great amazement.

(Mark 5:39-42 NKJV)

Jesus Healed All

You will notice through all of these accounts that Jesus healed all who came to Him, whether they had diseases, severe pain, demon possessed, those having seizures, even the paralysed were not disappointed.

It is interesting to see that people were more spiritually aware of those with demonic problems than we are today, in our sophisticated Western world. Sadly, people today will go to mediums or local spiritualist meetings for their spiritual comfort rather than looking to the Church.

We have looked mainly at the areas of healing, but Jesus also dealt with the demonic in various ways and methods. We know that Jesus did not seek out the demonised, so neither should we. He only dealt with those brought to Him or those who came to His attention.

Although the methods varied within the ministry that Jesus carried out, the results in every situation of deliverance were that the evil spirits within individual lives were always cast out:

Then He went down to Capernaum, a city of Galilee, and was teaching them on the Sabbaths. And they were astonished at His teaching, for His word was with authority. Now in the synagogue there was a man who had a spirit of an unclean demon. And he cried out with a loud voice, saying, "Let us alone! What have we to do with You, Jesus of Nazareth? Did You come to destroy us? I know You, who You are - the Holy One of God!"

But Jesus rebuked him, saying, "Be quiet, and come out of him!" And when the demon had thrown him in their midst, it came out of him. So they were all amazed and spoke among themselves, saying, "What a word this is! For with authority and power He commands the unclean spirits, and they come out."

(Luke 4:31-36 NKJV)

Be Quiet and Come Out!

It is interesting to see that Satan and his followers *(evil spirits)* do not have any trouble in recognising Jesus for who He was and is. But Jesus would in no way fellowship or hold any form of conversation with this demonic presence, but simply directly said, "Be quiet!" taking His authority and commanding this demon to "Come out of him!" In response to this, the demon threw the man down before the congregation, but without injuring the man in any way.

It is an important point that when we get involved in deliverance, no matter how dramatic the manifestations of the enemy within a person's life, the result will be complete healing and wholeness.

Healing and wholeness are the end result of a successful expulsion of a demon or demons. We also see that Jesus was in no way deterred from ministering in public, especially on the Sabbath, *(Sunday as we know it from a Christian point of view)*.

He was not concerned for the well being or the protection of those who were watching, who may have found the situation difficult to handle. The only concern of Jesus was that this man should be freed from his slavery. His heart was to bind the enemy and to loose the captives.

Clarity is the Hallmark of Christ

On another occasion, again on a Sabbath in Luke 13:15-16 we see Jesus telling those in the synagogue that they were nothing but hypocrites! Why? Because He said,

> *Doesn't each of you on the Sabbath untie his ox or donkey from the stall and lead it out to give it water? Then should not this woman, a daughter of Abraham, whom Satan has kept bound for eighteen long years, be set free (or loosed) on the Sabbath day from what bound her?*
>
> *(Luke 13:15-16)*

The result of this ministry on the Sabbath was one of humiliation for those in leadership but delight and joy from the congregation at seeing the wonderful things that Jesus was doing.

It would seem from scripture that Jesus was able to cast out demons from a distance. This occurred when a parent or someone in authority over servants, came in an attitude of faith, to receive on behalf of the one in their care, as with the Syro-Phoenician Woman *(Mark 7:24-30)*.

Names of demons were also demanded on occasions *(Mark 5:1-13)*. On entering the region of the Gerasenes and stepping out of the boat, Jesus was met by a man with an evil spirit who came from the tombs where he lived. No one could bind this man any more, not even with a chain. Night and day he would wander throughout the tombs and hillsides, crying out and cutting himself with stones, but then on seeing Jesus from a distance, ran and fell on his knees in front of Him.

Demons Speak through Man

Again we see an evil force speaking through a man recognising that this is Jesus Son of the Most High God. Jesus said a very interesting thing, He asked the demon, *"What is your name?"* This suggests to me that this demon at first did not obey the command of Jesus. Does this mean then that at this point Jesus was not successful with His command? Why would He need to ask the demon's name if He had already come out of the man? Jesus persisted and commanded the demon to answer, *"My name is Legion," he replied, "For we are many."*

Jesus, on His first command, referred to an individual evil spirit. But then when Jesus asked the spirit's name, He found out that He was not dealing with just one evil spirit, but many. The leader of this group of evil spirits within this man then began to beg or even try to bargain with Jesus. Why? Because these evil spirits did not want to wander through the wilderness without a body through whom they could manifest, *(Matthew 12:43)*.

The second choice for any evil spirit if there is not a human body for them to inhabit, is that of an animal – in this case, pigs. Jesus gave these spirits permission to enter a lower form of life than ourselves. The result was the total destruction of two thousand pigs, for it would seem that death was inevitable. **Again the man who was "possessed" was completely free, in his right mind,** suggesting that he was without any side effects, emotionally or otherwise, from such an affliction upon his life.

Forbidding them Re-entrance

Jesus, on other occasions, commanded demons never to return, forbidding them to enter or possess again *(Mark 9:14-27).*

From childhood, a boy had been afflicted with an evil spirit. From the description in this scripture it would seem to suggest that he could possibly be suffering from epileptic fits as well as being deaf and dumb. Jesus ordered the demon:

I command you, come out of him and never enter him again.

(Mark 9:25)

Jesus said, "never enter him again," because He knew that the demon or demons, which had been cast out, would for a time go through arid places seeking rest, seeking another body to inhabit. If they cannot find one they will try to return to the house that they left, *(Matthew 12:43-45).*

When an unclean spirit goes out of a man, he goes through dry places, seeking rest, and finds none. Then he says, "I will return to my house from which I came." And when he comes, he finds it empty, swept, and put in order. Then he goes and takes with him seven other spirits more wicked than himself, and they enter and dwell there; and the last state of that man is worse than the first. So shall it also be with this wicked generation.

(Matthew 12:43-45 NKJV)

We can see from this scripture that the final condition of that man, woman or child will be far worse than in the beginning. People in the church often say that deliverance is not for the body of Christ, for they believe that a Christian cannot have an evil spirit, afflicting their bodies.

Deliverance the Children's Bread

When reading the above scripture, it would seem to suggest that if I ministered deliverance to a non-believer, because of an affliction of some kind, then cast the evil spirit out, the pathway would remain open if that person did not give their life to Jesus Christ. There would be nothing in the body to keep the body free from the evil spirits that would possibly try to return and enter the body again. So their condition will be far worse than before.

The only way for a person to remain free of evil spirits is to accept Jesus Christ as their Saviour and Lord. We need to renew our minds so that we can then stand on the truth of scripture to be able to withstand the onslaught and attack of the demonic realm *(1 Peter 5:8)*.

A Christian can remain free through the Blood of Jesus and the power of the Holy Spirit. An unregenerate man or woman in the world most certainly cannot.

❖

PART THREE

The Intrusion of Demons

❖

CHAPTER 10

Our Perspective of the Temple

I need to re-affirm that I do not believe that a Christian can be demon possessed. To be possessed means to be completely taken over – spirit, soul and body – by the devil. I do believe however, that a Christian can be oppressed, remembering that there are degrees of "oppression" and "possession." I will not be discussing whether evil spirits inhabit or invade non-believers; but our attention will be focussed on this question:

Can a Christian have a Demon?

John Wimber said; "A Christian cannot be demon possessed because this implies ownership. We are born of God and have His Spirit living within us. 'Affliction, oppression, bondage and stronghold,' are words used to describe demonization of a lesser extent. This is much more common. This implies varying degrees of demonic influence in certain areas of a person's life. This can be linked to a military invasion of a city - even while the friendly forces occupy and control the city, isolated areas can remain under enemy dominion e.g. a deaf and dumb spirit *(Mark 9:25)*, a spirit of seduction or deceiving spirits *(1 Timothy 4:1)*.

Christians can be demonized on these levels of influence if they allow themselves to be *(1 Corinthians 10:20-22; 2 Corinthians 10:4-5; 1 Timothy 4:1-3)*. See 1 John 5:18-19 for the security of the believer."[1]

Five Old Testament Illustrations

One:

Saul was a believer *(1 Samuel 10:9)* but God changed Saul's heart. To argue that Saul was not a believer is to argue that God's Spirit would anoint an unbeliever *(10:1)*, and that God would anoint an unbeliever to rule over His inheritance.

Two:

Furthermore, the Holy Spirit came upon him and he joined the prophets and began prophesying *(1 Samuel 10:9-13)*.

Three:

Later, Saul fell into sin and was then tormented by an evil spirit sent from the Lord *(16:14)*. Does this mean then that God would directly use an evil force to bring a sinful man to repentance? Some would suggest that God's Holy Spirit and gifts are irreversible even though the person who has fallen into sin had previously moved powerfully under the anointing of God.

The reason why Saul was invaded by demons is not directly indicated. It may be however that his rebellion against God, which is likened to divination *(witchcraft)* was the cause *(1 Samuel 15:23)*. The consequence of Saul's rebellion was that the Spirit of the Lord departed from him and he was then handed over by God to the tormentor.

Four:

You will note that after David entered Saul's service and played his harp, worshipping with Psalms, Saul would find release from his torment. The evil spirit would leave him for a short time whilst David worshipped his God. I believe the reason for this is that when we worship God, this in turn will bring down His anointing. For God says that He will inhabit our praises and His hand will come upon us *(2 Kings 3:15)*.

I know from experience that when we get caught up in such anointed worship, those with demonic problems will feel very uncomfortable. Evil spirits cannot stay in the presence of God. They will either flee, causing the person to run out of the room or cause a manifestation; the evil spirit will then need to be cast out. *(Manifestations are evil spirits demonstrating their particular nature through a person, in a variety of ways).* In Saul's case, evil spirits left voluntarily *(1 Samuel 16:23).*

Five:

Some of the characteristics of Saul's demonization may have been:

- Anger *(1 Samuel 18:8)*
- Murder *(1 Samuel 18:10-11)*
- Fear *(1 Samuel 18:12, 29)*
- Suicide *(1 Samuel 31:4)* – a spirit of death

Four New Testament Illustrations

One:

A daughter of Abraham *(Luke 13:10-17)*. This unnamed lady was a believer *(13:16)*, called a "daughter of Abraham." Luke 19:9 indicates that a "son of Abraham" was one who had received salvation, which was pronounced by Jesus Himself. Paul makes it clear in Galatians 3:7 that those who believe are "children of Abraham." As we know from scripture this woman had an evil spirit for eighteen years, which crippled her *(Luke 13:11)*, bound by Satan *(v16)*. Jesus delivered her in the midst of criticism *(v13)* and set her free *(v12-16)*.

Two:

Judas, one of the twelve, *(Luke 22:3)*. Luke informs us at the beginning of chapter 22 that Satan entered Judas, a believer. We know he was with Jesus all through His three and a half years of ministry. He was in charge of the finances,

He was a thief; as keeper of the money bag, he used to help himself to what was put into it.

(John 12:6)

We know that he had a relationship with Jesus and was sent out with the other disciples to minister, he must have cast out demons, healed the sick, and preached the gospel *(Luke 9:1-6).*

He saw all the miraculous signs that were happening through their ministry at the time, and yet his heart was one of greed *(John 12:5).* He fell into sin and then Satan entered him.

Three:

Ananias and Sapphira, *(Acts 5:1-11)* were part of the "believers," mentioned in Acts. Deceit was not going to interrupt the progress of God's people. For scripture tells us that Ananias had let Satan fill his heart.

Now to me, if Satan fills your heart, he is coming into your body. He has to come in, to fill you. Ananias was a believer and must have, at some point, been Spirit filled and yet Satan was able to penetrate – able to come into his body.

Four:

A man was delivered to Satan *(1 Corinthians 5:1-5)* because of the practice of incest. Without the desire to be delivered, they were carrying on enjoying the flesh. The result was to be turned over into the realm of Satan so that the flesh could then be destroyed and the spiritual man saved. Very often someone has to be turned over to Satan, so that they can come to the end of themselves, before they turn back to God.

Evil spirits can inhabit the body of a Christian. The explanation of how this is possible is based primarily on a clear understanding of the difference between SPIRIT – SOUL – BODY.

❖

CHAPTER 11

Spirit, Soul & Body

Scripture teaches that prior to our salvation experience, we were spiritually dead because of our trespasses and sins. For when we followed the ways of the world, we were of the world, *(Ephesians 2:1).*

We were physically alive and were living out an earthly existence but we were dead spiritually. Our main interests were the cravings of our sinful nature and following its desires and thoughts. At this time we would not have had any perception of divine mysteries.

> *The person without the Spirit does not accept the things that come from the Spirit of God but considers them foolishness, and cannot understand them because they are discerned only through the Spirit.*
>
> *(1 Corinthians 2:14)*

Our new birth experience *(salvation)*, brings about a remedy for the condition of a man.

For God so loved the world that he gave his one and only Son, Jesus.

(John 3:16)

The Need to be Born Again

For His purpose is that all mankind may have eternal life. To bring this about Jesus tells us that no one can see the kingdom of God unless he is born again *(John 3:3-7)*. He goes on to explain this experience by stating that flesh gives birth to flesh, but the Spirit gives birth to spirit. This happens when we hear the Word of Truth, the Gospel of our Salvation.

Having believed, you were marked in him with a seal, the promised Holy Spirit, who is the deposit guaranteeing our inheritance.

(Ephesians 1:13-14)

Our spirit is then quickened – made alive – by the Holy Spirit coming in. Now, in this new position, we are not just physically existing, but also spiritually alive. Jesus comes into our human experience and brings in His Life. By accepting the life of Christ, we take Him as Lord, then give Him control of the physical, emotional and mental condition of our lives.

You however, are controlled not by the sinful nature but by the Spirit, if the Spirit of God lives in you. And if anyone does not have the Spirit of Christ, he does not belong to Christ...

But if by the Spirit you put to death the misdeeds of the body, you will live, because those who are lead by the Spirit of God, are sons of God...

The Spirit himself testifies with our spirits that we are God's children.

(Romans 8:9, 13-14, 16)

The Indwelling Spirit

From this, we see that the Holy Spirit indwells the human spirit at the time of salvation. But then we see quite clearly that the rest of our body has to be brought into obedience. This very often takes a lifetime, for we are to put off the old self and put on the new *(Colossians 3:5-17)*. There is also clear indication that the spirit, soul and body of a man are three separate parts.

May God himself, the God of peace, sanctify you through and through. May your whole spirit, soul and body be kept blameless at the coming of our Lord Jesus Christ.

(1 Thessalonians 5:23)

We need to establish that man is a spirit who possesses a soul and lives in a body. It is our spirit that receives salvation, the Holy Spirit giving birth to the human spirit. It is only at this point that we can then begin to fellowship with God, for God is a Spirit and He made man to fellowship with Him.

We as the threefold man are to be preserved without blame at the coming of the Lord, for when the Lord comes, this whole man – spirit soul and body – will be preserved. We have a new spirit now, but we will have a new body at the coming of the Lord Jesus Christ *(1 Corinthians 15:35-38).* At the moment though, we are outwardly wasting away, our bodies are, as we grow older, deteriorating. Yet inwardly we are being renewed day by day, by the power and strength of the Holy Spirit *(2 Corinthians 4:16).*

Paul goes on to say:

> *For our light and momentary troubles are achieving for us an eternal glory that far outweighs them all. So we fix our eyes not on what is seen, but on what is unseen. For what is seen is temporary, but what is unseen is eternal.*
>
> *(2 Corinthians 4:17-18)*

We may go through trials from a natural standpoint, but these things are just for a moment in time. For we can look forward to something far more wonderful and lasting, an eternal future. For we are not to look upon the now or the seen, as Smith Wigglesworth once said, ***"I am not moved by what I see. I am not moved by what I feel. I am moved only by what I believe."***

Sacrifices, Holy and Pleasing

The second part of our make-up is our soul, the intellect, emotions and will. It is the part of us that reasons and thinks in readiness to make decisions. The soul then deals with the mental realm. In Romans 12:1, Paul tells us, *(the real us – the spirit man)* to:

> *Offer your bodies as living sacrifices, Holy and pleasing to God – this is your spiritual act of worship.*
>
> *(Romans 12:1)*

Then Paul goes on to say in regards to our minds, intellect or our soul, stating:

> *Do not conform any longer to the pattern of this world, but be transformed by the renewing of your mind. Then you will be able to test and approve what God's will is – His good, pleasing and perfect will.*
>
> *(Romans 12:2)*

Be Responsible for the House

Thirdly, the body is the outward man, the physical, the house in which we live. We are totally responsible for our bodies, not God. We have been given the position of caretaker of the temple that He has created, for He tells us to present ourselves as living sacrifices, holy, acceptable to God *(Romans 12:1)*.

This would suggest that we need to take care of our bodies physically *(1 Timothy 4:8)*, with exercise and well balanced diet. Our bodies should in no way dictate to us. They are not meant to take control by their cravings or lusting after worldly desires, but are to be taken into subjection to what the Spirit wills. God does not want us to be carnal Christians ruled by our bodies, for we need to run the race in order to receive the crown that will last forever.

Paul says:

> *Therefore I do not run like a man running aimlessly; I do not fight like a man beating the air. No, I beat my body and make it my slave so that after I have preached to others, I myself will not be disqualified for the prize.*
>
> *(1 Corinthians 9:26-27)*

Now we have discovered as Christians that we live inside a body, does this mean that we take up the whole of our bodies or does the real us *(Spirit filled)*, which is born-again exist just within the heart of a man? It is obvious from our discoveries that we are, "one" yet three parts.

Remember, the question in this chapter is, "Can a Christian have a demon indwelling his body?" We need to look more closely at *how* an evil spirit can dwell within the body.

The bible makes it quite clear that we are the temple of the Holy Spirit.

> *Don't you know that you yourselves are God's temple and that God's Spirit lives in you? If anyone destroys God's temple, God will destroy him; for God's temple is sacred, and you are that temple.*
>
> *(1 Corinthians 3:16-17)*

To take this issue further and understand some simple basic facts about the temple that we now live in, we need to look at two illustrations. This will help us understand how evil spirits can interfere with the running of the temple in which the Christian now lives and shares with the living God.

Two Illustrations

Firstly, the Temple of Jerusalem was constructed in the same way as the tabernacle that Moses had erected in the wilderness. For God's desire was to dwell among His people *(Exodus 25:8)*. God Himself showed Moses the design when he was forty days with God on Mount Sinai *(Exodus 24:18)*. As you can see from the example below it consisted of three parts:

First illustration - The Temple of Jerusalem:

- **The Holy of Holies:** The most sacred place, entered only once a year by the high priest
- **The Holy Place:** Separated from the Holy of Holies by a linen curtain
- **The Courtyard:** The Courtyard stood at the west end of the temple

The second illustration is of man. When talking about destroying the temple, Jesus was talking about Himself *(Matthew 26:61)*. We also know that scriptures talk about us being temples, and tents *(2 Corinthians 5:1-5)*, *(we are the tent/ temple that God has now chosen to live in)*.

We can see from the first illustration that once the temple was built, God was at last able to dwell with His people, but He was still separate, even though He desired to be intimate with man. We can see from this second illustration, that intimacy with God now exits. At the time of the crucifixion the veil within the temple was torn from top to bottom *(Mark 15:38)*.

Since we have confidence to enter the Most Holy Place by the blood of Jesus, by a new and living way opened for us through the curtain, that is, his body.

(Hebrews 10:19-20)

Jesus made it possible for us to become the temple that God has now chosen to dwell in. And this temple also has three parts, SPIRIT – SOUL – BODY.

Second illustration is of man:

- The spirit being the Holy of Holies
- The soul being the Holy Place
- The body being the Courtyard

There is a thin dividing line between each section:

This goes along with the Old Testament view of the temple. But we also need to remember the dramatic incident that took place in the temple at Jerusalem. This we find recorded in John 2:14.

In the temple courts He found men selling cattle, sheep, and doves and others sitting at tables exchanging money. So He made a whip out of cord, and drove everyone from the temple.

Disruptive Influences

It is interesting to see that Jesus drove from the temple courts disruptive influences that should not have been there, treating it like a cattle market and abusing the temple.

The traders were not sitting in the most Holy of Holies, they were sitting in the outer court. We know that the men selling cattle, and others exchanging money, were confined to the courtyard.

But they would have been interfering with the running of the temple, causing an invasion in someway. They were not in the Holy Place and certainly not in the Holy of Holies, for if they had entered the Holy of Holies they would have been *(in theory)* struck down dead, *(Numbers 4:17-20; Exodus 28:35-43; Leviticus 16:2).*

Remember, they were still in the temple! Now take this as a parallel to the temple that God now lives in. The courtyard being the body of a believer. All those interfering with the running of the temple in Jerusalem needed to be driven out. In the same way Jesus desires to drive out any interference caused by evil spirits, which are within the courtyard of our bodies.

Demons cannot enter our spirit *(The Holy of Holies)*, that which is born again and which receives the baptism of the Holy Spirit. The spirit is filled, but the body and soul can be invaded, infected by disease or evil spirits. For evil spirits like those selling cattle or exchanging money, will interfere with the running of the temple in which God now dwells.

Evil spirits, which have a foothold or control of our emotions, mind or sexual desires, will cause us to be disobedient and cause us to lust after the things of the world. Their aim is to cause total destruction to man, which in turn brings separation from God.

Removing Trespassing spirits

Deliverance is to remove trespassing spirits from the body of a believer, in order that Jesus can reign over these areas as well. Jesus has made adequate provision for the whole man, but part of the responsibility rests upon us, as is shown in the following scripture:

> *Work out your salvation with fear and trembling for it is God who works in you to will and to act according to his purpose.*
>
> *(Philippians 2:12-13)*

To the believer, it is said that God is at work in you, but the salvation spoken of is not completed. It needs to be, **"worked out."** Jesus walked constantly with His eyes on the Father, so as the Father spoke to His Son, the spirit within Jesus was obedient to the Spirit of God. Jesus was not obedient to His own will or emotions but the will of the Father.

> *Going a little further, He fell to the ground and prayed that if possible the hour might pass from Him. Abba, Father, he said, everything is possible for you. Take this cup from me. Yet not what I will, but what you will.*
>
> *(Mark 14:35-36)*

There are times when what I perceive in my mind is not always truth, that is why I have to go by what the Holy Spirit is telling me. This then becomes my way of life, as it was with Jesus, for it is not my will but the Father's will that counts.

CHAPTER 12

Entry Points for Demonic Influences

Sin was the cause of the fall of man *(Genesis 3:1-24)*. God created us in His own image and His intention and purpose for creating us was for relationship and fellowship.

Because of the deception in the Garden of Eden, Adam and Eve fell into sin, their relationship with God was broken. Without this relationship between man and God, peace and security of life was lost. We know that salvation is the only way to bring a remedy, where man and God can once more have the relationship that He intended.

Lucifer, before being thrown out of Heaven, was in perfect unity with God but because of his pride he fell into sin and rebelled against God, His authority and order. *Sin is rebellion and refusal of order and authority.* We know that in the world, when a man refuses the authority of a Sovereign God, he becomes his own authority. Men also, at times, reject the authority of governments, which are trying to bring about social order. Within our lives, we need order and justice to function in the way God intended *(Romans 13:1-6).*

Where does this Rebellion come From?

We notice rebellion very often within our own children. Where does this rebellion come from? I believe it comes from our fallen nature. We can overcome this rebellion by discipline, *(the laying on of hands, starting at the bottom!)* For we know that if this rebellion carries on, disorder and disunity amongst the family would occur. In scripture God tells our children to obey, submitting under the authority of the parents.

> *That it may go well with you and that you may enjoy long life on the earth...*
>
> *(Ephesians 6:1-4)*

God's intention is that we enjoy life, but how can we enjoy life if we are not submissive to authority.

When a person rebels against God's given authority, he is walking in sin *(Romans 13:1-7)*. This in turn, if prolonged, will leave the door open for Satan to afflict him with his evil desires, which is to totally control man.

So a man or woman who will not submit to the authority of God will begin to become slaves to the temptation and deception of their own bodies. They will believe the desires of their flesh and the perversion and fantasies of their mind and be lead into deception. We need to be careful not to become slaves to sin, for this can only lead to death.

> *Don't you know that when you offer yourselves to someone to obey him as slaves, you are slaves to the one whom you obey – whether you are slaves to sin, which leads to death, or to obedience which leads to righteousness? But thanks be to God that, though you used to be slaves to sin, you wholeheartedly obeyed the form of teaching to which you were entrusted.*
>
> (Romans 6:16-17)

Sin then, is a choice, and if not dealt with can become a habit, which in turn will lead to bondage. Open doors give evil spirits the opportunity to tempt, deceive, accuse, condemn, pressure, defile, resist, oppose, control, steal, afflict, kill and destroy. The only way to be free of Satan and his evil devices is to receive Jesus Christ as Lord and Saviour.

Crucify the Flesh

But for many Christians it would seem that even after their born-again experience, rebellion still needs to be dealt with. Sometimes it would seem that this can only be done by being turned over to the flesh, for we need to crucify the sinful nature *(Galatians 5:19-21)*. If this action is not taken by us then it will be taken by God.

> *As obedient children, do not conform to the evil desires you had when you lived in ignorance. But just as he who called you is holy so be holy in all you do; for it is written: Be holy, because I am holy.*
>
> (1 Peter 1:14-16)

Failure to turn from our rebellious ways can only result in us being delivered into the hands of Satan, so that the sinful nature – the flesh – can be destroyed and the spirit man saved *(1 Corinthians 5:1-5)*.

Doors Opened by Sin

Sin has dramatic results upon our lives. Doors that have been opened by sin can affect our lives for many years.

I remember a situation that God lead me into some years ago. Past sin was the cause of the problems that a particular woman *(even though she had been a Christian for some years)*, was going through.

It all started with a telephone call, which sent me flying out to a foreign land where I was a guest in a very expensive villa. The Christian couple with whom I was staying, worked for the owner. I wondered why God would send me hundreds of miles to minister to this couple when they were themselves involved in a deliverance and healing ministry.

When I arrived the lady told me that at nights in her bedroom, there was a feeling of death, which got so bad that she even felt like committing suicide. She did not know what was wrong or why this was happening.

I spent two days waiting for the right time, for God to direct me, on the third day we sat down and started talking. I began to pray for her. She was sitting on a chair outside in the sunshine, with nothing on her feet, she seemed very relaxed.

Suddenly I noticed her toes and fingers were twisting and distorting, her legs and arms drawing backwards, she was turning blue with pain and began to look like an old woman. She started to say in a shallow voice "Help me! Help me! It hurts." I found it hard to believe such manifestations.

Surprising myself, I began to say, "In the Name of Jesus I command you spirit of arthritis, crippling spirit, spirit of death, come out of her," but nothing happened! She was hurting so much from these dramatic manifestations that I knew she needed to relax, even if it was just for a few moments. I spoke peace to her body in the Name of Jesus and the distortions ceased.

Her body went back to its normal state, her fingers and toes straightened, colour came back into her body. It would have been easy to think that she had been delivered, for the manifestations had gone, but in my spirit I knew this was not so.

Some Years Previous

I asked her whether there was anything in her past that would allow Satan to afflict her in this way. We prayed once more and God brought to mind a situation some years previously, when she had worked as a nurse in a nursing home for elderly people. The majority of patients were suffering with arthritis and crippling diseases, because of their age they were at the point of death.

This lady admitted that at that particular time, she did not care about anyone but herself. She treated the patients cruelly, missing their medications and deliberately quickened their oncoming deaths. This sin, opened up the way for her to be afflicted by evil spirits.

In some cases God will bring to mind past sin in this way, so that repentance can be brought about. Then complete freedom from evil spirits can occur. These evil spirits had a right to be there because of this unrepented sin, yet this woman was a Spirit filled Christian.

Maybe God had to bring her to this particular place and time within her life where she could be finally freed from this sin and affliction. With her repentance, God's power came on me and I said, "In the Name of Jesus I command you evil spirits to go." With that she shrivelled up as she had before and leapt out of the chair onto the ground with a shriek. I knew then that the demons were gone.

Emotional Trauma

There are many other ways that Satan can find a way of penetrating our beings. Emotional trauma is caused by violence and emotional shock and can have lasting effects. For instance, if someone has a back problem or some other related illness, there could be a spirit of infirmity. I usually ask in these instances whether the person has been at some time involved in a car accident or an accident of some kind, where for a split second they were unconscious, for this can allow a spirit of infirmity or fear to come in.

Another avenue where a spirit of fear can come in is if a person has been severely frightened in some way, for example a near drowning experience that brings on the fear of water or being attacked by a dog that brings a fear for dogs.

Grief

Grief is another example where Satan can get a foothold. Someone in the family may have died and you now feel that your world has come to an end. Grief and loneliness in these situations can easily overpower us.

This is an area in many people's lives, which needs healing so that they can release the dead person, for if this loved one is not released, it can encourage the affliction of familiar spirits. *(Familiar spirits are evil spirits that will manifest themselves as your loved ones who have died)*. In turn, this will cause depression, grief, loneliness and despair.

Mediums and Familiar Spirits

Instead of turning to Jesus, many at this time try to hold on to their loved ones by going to mediums and such, where they will then try to relate to their loved ones. This can only lead to bondage.

> *Give no regard to mediums and familiar spirits; do not seek after them, to be defiled by them: I am the Lord your God.*
>
> *(Leviticus 19:31 NKJV)*

> *Let no one be found among you who sacrifices his son or daughter in the fire, who practises divination or sorcery, interprets omens, engages in witchcraft, or casts spells,*

*or who is a medium or spiritist or who consults the dead.
Anyone who does these things is detestable to the Lord,
and because of these detestable practices the Lord your
God will drive out those nations before you. You must be
blameless before the Lord your God.*

(Deuteronomy 18:10-13)

Corrie Ten Boom said, "After the war in Germany
there was among many people great uncertainty about
the soldiers that were missing. Were they still in Russian
concentration camps, or had they died during the fighting?
This uncertainty caused great suffering among their relatives,
and many people went to fortune-tellers, to find out about
their loved ones. I do not know whether they got any real
information, but this I know, many came to me and told me
about permanent darkness in their hearts and an urge to
commit suicide. This symptom is always a sure evidence of
demon influence!"[1]

Miscarriage

Miscarriage is an area of gross misunderstanding. We
are told that when this occurs we can easily try again. They
forget that this was a life created in the womb, whether this
child was three months developed or full term is irrelevant.

God tells us that He knew each of us before we were
born,

*For you created my inmost being you knit me together in
my mother's womb... My frame was not hidden from you
when I was made in the secret place...*

(Psalm 139:13, 15)

Many women find that they grieve for this lost child and that they often wonder whether the baby was a boy or a girl and how he or she would have looked.

At one time I was ministering in Germany when a woman was brought to me who was depressed. There seemed to be a cloud of heaviness surrounding her. It was difficult to speak to her directly as I don't speak German but by using an interpreter, we were able to relate in a small measure. As we prayed, the Lord revealed to me that she had several miscarriages, although she did have three growing children. But her desire was to have a big family, so the more children she lost, the more she fell into grief and despair.

What she did to compensate the loss of these children was to buy "dolls" in their place. Each doll was dressed as a new born child, she also named them. This became such an obsession that it took over her whole life. This in itself would have opened the way for familiar spirits, causing complete confusion, depression and in turn, more miscarriages.

She needed to give these lost children over to God and to let the dolls go. She knew this was the only way she could be free to go on in life.

A Fetus being Aborted

A woman at another meeting came up to me and asked whether I could pray for her heart condition. As I began to pray for her she fell to the ground and curled up as in a fetal position. I realised that this was no ordinary heart condition, for the manifestations were of a fetus being aborted. In these circumstances I might add, I never know what to do!

I knelt beside her and prayed earnestly that God would show me what to do. The woman was not in a state where I could ask questions. I needed to hear God in this situation, "Lord, Help!"

The Lord showed me that when she was being created in her mother's womb, maybe forty-five years previously, that her mother was going through a difficult time. It was just after the war, poverty and stress would have been dominant. A woman in these circumstances did not really want to be pregnant for many reasons.

One likely example would have been money, whether she could afford a child at that time. I carried on praying, "Lord show me what to do." I felt the Lord was saying that during the time when this woman was being carried within her mother's womb, she had been afflicted with rejection, anger, despair and death.

You see, when a woman is pregnant and begins to hate the fact that she is carrying a child, her body is capable of responding to her will. Her body may try to abort, rejecting the fetus and causing, in some cases, a full miscarriage.

In other instances, children, unwanted during the mother's pregnancy can end up with many problems. Sometimes they face rejection throughout their lives, hatred towards their mothers, problems in their own marriages, where miscarriages can take place or even as in this woman's case, a heart condition.

Prayer for forgiveness towards her mother needed to take place, repenting of wrong attitudes. Obviously the spirits, which were there had to be cast out and a healing had to take place.

Promiscuous Society

In today's promiscuous society it is considered normal for men and women to have sexual relationships outside of marriage, thus creating unhealthy relationships or soul ties. *(Please refer to the book, Sexual Madness, In a Sexually Confused World, co-written with my wife Jennifer).*[2]

They do not realise the harm that they are opening themselves up to. Scripture clearly states that when a man and woman come together they become one flesh *(Matthew 19:5-6).*

Usually men and women are looking for love in these relationships, because often, love is the missing element. Many feel rejected and are looking for love and acceptance, turning to ungodly relationships which give them a sense of approval, emotional strength and sometimes a reason for existence. Those who have had a promiscuous past occasionally need cutting off from their past relationships otherwise problems can occur later on within marriage.

Ancestry (Blood lines)

Many are living in what they believe has came down through their blood line. But God tells those of us who are being obedient to His will that, *"He chooses our inheritance for us" (Psalm 47:4).* But sadly many of us believe Satan and his lies.

How many of us have listened to a family member or even a doctor telling us that our particular sickness is inherited. Doesn't this put us into bondage, as the tree of knowledge would so easily entangle and cause us to sin, by deceiving us from the truth of God's Word?

Satan has been nothing but a liar from the very beginning *(John 8:44)*. Job, who did not sin, fell into the trap of fear and what he feared came upon him *(Job 3:25)*.

Recently my father died, at the age of fifty-six. He had been ill for many years with depression and other related illnesses. He died very unexpectedly, after a massive heart attack. Since that time fear has run rampant through my family – my brothers and sister have all been for check-ups at the doctors. One of my brothers has even taken up marathon running, to overcome any future development of heart trouble. But I praise God that He has chosen me as a son and I have a full inheritance, for the Lord came that we may have life and have it to the full *(John 10:10)*.

The Blood, The Blood

I remember also a situation not so long ago, in Hereford, were I was asked to go and minister to a woman. As we were praying, I felt within my spirit that I should cut her off from her blood-line, which came down through her father. As I lifted my hand in response to the command I said, "In the Name of Jesus I cut you off from the blood-line of your father." Even before I had finished this command, she dramatically became delirious, she began crying out *"the blood, the blood."*

She was not calling on the Blood of Jesus, but she was seeing a vision of the massacre of men during the second world war which her father had gone through.

She was reliving the grief and torment that her father must have felt and taken upon himself. He obviously found his circumstances so horrific that this opened him up to the demonic realm. This spirit of grief and sorrow tormented him, but manifested within her, at birth. Over the years she had wondered why grief was so apparent in her own life through years of loneliness and despair. She eventually married and was happy for a time.

The problem seemed to ease but then resurfaced with the death of her husband. She began grieving, becoming bitter because of her circumstances, resentment set in towards others who were happy or content, and towards God, blaming Him for her circumstances.

The only way that she could find release from all of this, was to find the ability to forgive. The Lord, by His amazing grace, found a way to bring about a situation where someone could come along and stand in the gap with her, bringing about complete freedom and inner peace. Nothing is impossible for God.

Curses

Many of the above situations could be described as curses. Curses upon families and individuals are quite common, but we have a provision made for us through the sacrificial death of Jesus, clearly stated by Paul in Galatians 3:13-14.

Christ redeemed us from the curse of the law by becoming a curse for us, for it is written: "Cursed is everyone who is hung on a tree." He redeemed us in order that the blessings given to Abraham might come to the Gentiles through Christ Jesus, so that by faith we might receive the promise of the Spirit.

Derek Prince in his booklet, "From Curse to Blessing" explains how a curse can operate in your life:

He says, "A curse is something like a dark shadow or an evil hand from the past oppressing you, pressing you down, holding you back, tripping you up, and propelling you in a direction you did not really wish to take. It is like a negative atmosphere that surrounds you, which seems to be stronger at some times than others, but from which you are never free.

If I were to choose one key word, it would be the word 'frustration.' For example, you reach a certain level of achievement or progress in your life and you seem to have all the needed qualifications for success, yet something goes wrong. You start over, you reach the same level, then something goes wrong again. This seems to be the pattern of your life and yet there is no obvious reason for it.

This pattern may occur in various areas: business, personal relationships *(especially marriage and family)*, a career, finance, or health. In all probability, whatever area it may be, that dark shadow or evil hand is a curse over your life, perhaps going back many generations."[3]

Don't Speak Negative Words

We need to be careful in the way we speak the words we say. It is easy to speak negative words that would bind those to whom they are spoken. This is commonplace within our families, for I know myself that words spoken in frustration by my parents and the teachers at school bound me to my circumstances. I found it very difficult to remember how to spell words; each week having to stand up in front of the class, trying to spell words that simply evaded my memory.

It is easy in these situations to call someone, "stupid or thick," so that the person begins to believe that they are stupid or thick. These negative words have brought about the fruit which they describe.

When ministering to a young woman who had been rejected by her mother, I found out that she had lived, *(not willingly but constantly)* listening to **negative and suggestive language.** As she became a teenager, her mother then began to accuse her of being a "flirt" and suggested that she would end up a "prostitute."

The end result was that she seemed to attract men, although this was never her desire. She was being spiritually manipulated to become a vehicle of Satan's perverse ways. The spirit of prostitution had been able to take refuge. On dealing with this issue, remembering that **repentance is the key to all deliverance,** she is now happily married and totally restored, as God intended.

Rejection

There is a little girl or little boy within all of us who needs to be loved and made secure in acceptance. The result of rejection within our lives is usually total despair. We need to understand that there are degrees of rejection and the effect differs from person to person.

Rejection comes from many different reactions to life and circumstances around us as we develop. This can happen before birth, with parents who cannot communicate love, maybe because they have suffered from rejection themselves.

Parents who have striven for success in life often find they have little or no time for their children. This inbuilt rejection from our early years can cause us to feel rejected during our school years and as we grow up into adult life.

Those who have been rejected often try to fill the emptiness in their lives by trying to gain acceptance through other means, such as an absorbing career, acquiring possessions, or throwing themselves into study. All these attitudes say, "I want to be noticed, admired, even praised." Stealing, lying and suicide are also tactics to gain love and attention.

The goal of the one who has been rejected is to receive love. It is easy for a person in these circumstances to become self-centred and want the world to revolve around them.

Permissive sex and homosexuality are ways a person will try to receive love and fulfilment. The sad dramatic result of all this is very often insecurity, loneliness, and self pity.

Because the person feels that no-one wants to love them, they will begin to wish that they had not been born. This in turn leads to self-rejection.

One thing that we can be thankful for is that Jesus bore our sorrow, grief and rejection, to free us from the chains that enslave us.

Isaiah 53:3 says,

> *He was despised and rejected by mankind, a man of suffering, and familiar with pain...*

This is our Lord and Saviour, He dealt with our rejection on the cross, He took our affliction and iniquities upon Himself. This then has brought total freedom, for Isaiah goes on to say in 54:4,

> *Do not be afraid; you will not suffer shame. Do not fear disgrace; you will not be humiliated. You will forget the shame of your youth and remember no more the reproach of your widowhood.*

The Lord also says in Jeremiah 30:17,

> *"But I will restore you to health and heal your wounds," declares the Lord, "because you are called an outcast, Zion for whom no-one cares."*

We need to accept that we are a new creation, the old has gone and the new has come *(2 Corinthians 5:17)*. For we are God's workmanship, created in Jesus Christ to do good works, which God prepared in advance for us to do *(Ephesians 2:10)*.

He predestined us to be adopted as His sons, for we are the ones He loves and because of His grace we have redemption through His Blood, the forgiveness of sins *(Ephesians 1:3-14).*

We need to forgive ourselves and others for the rejection of the past and receive the Father's love, for He would say to us,

> *I have loved you with an everlasting love; I have drawn you with loving-kindness. I will build you up again and you will be rebuilt, O Virgin Israel. Again you will take up your tambourines and go out to dance with the joyful. Again you will plant vineyards on the hills of Samaria; the farmers will plant them and enjoy their fruit.*
>
> *(Jeremiah 31:3-5)*

Bitterness Poisons Us

Most of us can accept to some degree, that bitterness is the cause of division within our relationships, for example our families, at work, school or even in church.

In Hebrews we read,

> *See to it that no-one misses the grace of God and that no bitter root grows up to cause trouble and defile many.*
>
> *(Hebrews 12:15)*

No bitter root should be allowed to grow within our lives, but the fact is that many of us at some time have been bruised. We had the experience of falling from a tree like an apple, at first the shock of bouncing to the ground was deflected, shaken off. But some days or months later the bruise began to show, like an apple we begin to rot with bitterness. We poison ourselves and everyone who surrounds us, because of our attitudes and the things that we begin to say.

Others pick up the bitterness that we have and they too become polluted *(Hebrews 12:15)*. We then blame other people because we have become bitter. The bitterness becomes hatred. This then is the opening that Satan uses to afflict us with evil spirits and diseases.

For those who have been bitter over the years, sometimes that bitterness expresses itself in crippling arthritis. Forgiveness towards those who have hurt us, for whatever reason, needs to take place. Then healing can be brought about.

Forgiveness is the Key

Forgiveness is the key to release bitterness, resentments and other negative emotions. We need not judge or condemn others for in so doing we will be condemned.

Forgive and you will be forgiven.

(Luke 6:37)

If we are not willing to forgive, forgiveness will not come our way. We have been forgiven of sin, our debt has been cancelled, yet we find it hard to forgive others *(Matthew 18:27)*.

We need to release our brothers and sisters from whatever they have done towards us. If we do not forgive we will become like them. The end result of unforgiveness is that we will be turned over to the jailer to be tortured *(Matthew 18:34)*. Forgiveness is the attitude of God and the example that we must follow. We might not feel like forgiving, but then we cannot go on our feelings, we need to be obedient to the Word of God.

Forgiveness then becomes an act of our will, WE CHOOSE TO FORGIVE:

For if you forgive men when they sin against you, your heavenly Father will also forgive you. But if you do not forgive men their sins, your Father will not forgive your sins.

(Matthew 6:14-15)

❖

CHAPTER 13

Involvement in Occult Practices

I want to briefly look at the involvement in the occult, which entangles and deceives many people. The bible denounces any and all occult practices.

When you enter the land the Lord your God is giving you, do not learn to imitate the detestable ways of the nations there. Let no-one be found among you who sacrifices his son or daughter in the fire, who practices divination or sorcery, interprets omens, engages in witchcraft, or casts spells, or who is a medium or spiritist or who consults the dead.

Anyone who does these things is detestable to the Lord and because of these detestable practices the Lord your God will drive out those nations before you. You must be blameless before the Lord your God.

(Deuteronomy 18:9-13)

The late Dr Carroll Thompson in his manual, "Possess the Land" says, "The ancient religions were rooted in the occult. These religions were called Mystery Religions because of secret rites experienced by the initiated. Babylon is thought to be the beginning place for such religions and their traditions. The bible describes the existence of a religious system in the end-times as, 'Mystery, Babylon The Great, The Mother of Harlots, and Abominations of the Earth' *(Revelation 17:5)*. The occult practices very easily fit into this description.

Hidden Secrets of the Occult

Man has discovered hidden secrets by which to open doors to the occult, these secrets are, 'the mysteries of Babylon.' God brought complete destruction to ancient Babylon *(Jeremiah 50)*, and Babylon's spiritual counterpart in the end-times awaits for the same destruction *(Revelation 19:2)*."[1]

The occult has its beginning in idolatry and will open the doors to hidden powers. These powers are demons *(Psalm 106:35-38; 1 Corinthians 10:20)*, and these demonic forces allow themselves to be used by the occult seeker.

They mingled with the nations and adopted their customs. They worshipped their idols, which became a snare to them. They sacrificed their sons and their daughters to demons. They shed innocent blood, the blood of their sons and daughters, whom they sacrificed to the idols of Canaan, and the land was desecrated by their blood. They

defiled themselves by what they did; by their deeds they
prostituted themselves.

(Psalm 106:35-39)

The price for such a service means the complete enslavement of the individual. Many are being entangled at a very young age, for many believe that no harm can come upon them. They believe that you can play around and have fun in these areas.

Involvement with the occult, whether it be tarot cards, ouija boards or spiritism will result in mental disorder, spiritual and physical damage to the body. Seemingly trivial activities such as horoscopes and Halloween parties can be part of that process.

Dr Chris Andrews Warns

"Involvement with the occult can lead to anything from depression and broken relationships to sexual deviation and murder."

Dr Andrews' view is born out of experience. He regularly deals with patients who have been hurt by their involvement with the supernatural and superstition.

"There are so many areas of potential contamination. I have had people coming to me with all sorts of different conditions."[2]

One situation we heard of, was a young girl of fourteen, who was normal and well balanced. She was persuaded by friends to play with an ouija board, the damage from this was instant. The next day she suffered a severe mental and nervous breakdown, she ended up being certified and sent to a mental hospital, where she stayed on and off for the next five years.

Over this time she had severe behavioural problems, becoming violent and difficult to handle. Each time her parents managed to persuade the authorities to allow her home, she would end up becoming violent and would have to be returned to the mental hospital.

It took five years to treat her and get her to the point where she could join society again. Not long after she was released she gave her life to the Lord and is now married, living a normal life.

Even in Italy where we currently live, the following article is conducive with what we have been discussing:

"Requests for the services of exorcists have tripled in Italy recently and the Vatican is laying on fresh training courses for aspiring Devil-fighters to cope with the demand, a veteran exorcist told Vatican Radio... There are now about half a million cases every year in Italy, Palermo priest Father Benigno Palilla said. He said much of the reason was that 'the number of people ready to go to magicians, witches, card and Tarot readers has greatly increased. By doing so they open the door to the Devil, and to possession.'"[3]

Tarot Cards to Black Magic

Dr Michael David has treated dozens of patients who have suffered because of their involvement with the occult.

"Such people are very often vague, generally miserable, anxious and discouraged without knowing why," he reports. "It is only when you dig into their history that you discover that they have been directly involved with things ranging from spiritism and tarot cards to the fringes of black magic," says Dr David.

Despite such evidence the occult is promoted as harmless. A large advertisement and reply coupon for a book on witchcraft in the respectable Exchange and Mart newspaper promised information on, "How to leave your physical body and travel invisibly," "Commanding things to happen through powerful spells and invocations," "The ultimate witchcraft ritual."

The Bishop of Thetford, the Right Reverend Timothy Dudley-Smith says, "God is Spirit and God is Love. But there are powers of darkness, malevolent spiritual forces; and to participate even on the fringes of the occult can do immense harm."

Dr Tony Dale, the General Secretary of Caring Professions Concern warns, "Trivial contact with the occult can lead to oppression, depression, schizophrenia and manifestations of epilepsy," and consultant child psychiatrist, Dr Graham Melville-Thomas has encountered cases where children have been damaged as a result of the occult.

"Involvement such as ouija boards are," he says, "potentially damaging and can unbalance children who are vulnerable."

"To such medical opinion, is added the full weight of the Children Medical Fellowship," declares its Secretary Dr Keith Saunders. "I am in touch with 20,000 doctors around the world who would say there is no doubt that involvement with spirits other than the Holy Spirit leads to suffering in body, mind and spirit."

Halloween, Harmless fun or Occult!

On the face of it, Halloween is just harmless, childish fun. It is an opportunity to dress up, play games and inflict, "trick or treat" on the neighbours. And it is probably true that no one who has been involved has ever suffered direct harm as a result. Yet an eminent Psychiatrist, Dr David Enoch, warns that despite its fun side, "Halloween is the periphery of something far more serious and it can place people in jeopardy."

Dr Enoch formerly Senior Consultant Psychiatrist at the Royal Liverpool Hospital and the University of Liverpool, UK states, "Halloween lends respectability to an occult world that can inflict forces into people's lives that they do not understand and often cannot combat."

As a child Audrey Harper used to call the matron of the children's home where she lived "a witch." She says, "I used to imagine her on a broomstick. That was the childhood picture I carried with me."

But in her early twenties, Audrey became personally involved with witchcraft and learned that modern day witches are far removed from storybook tales. She witnessed real spiritual powers being exercised by witches as they cast spells. On one occasion she witnessed death by heart attack of a previously healthy person who had been cursed.

Eventually Audrey herself became a witch. "I made a blood covenant with Lucifer." She began to learn signs, symbols and spells. "I also took part in the desecration of Christian Churches." She says, "People laugh at witches, they think it is all about old women on broomsticks, but it is one of the most dangerous things you could ever imagine. I lived for years in torment, we did some dreadful things and I tried to kill myself when I remembered what I had done."

30,000 Witches in Britain

Audrey is not an isolated case, estimates indicate that there are approximately 53,172 pagan/witches in Britain today.

Rev. Kevin Logan, a Church of England Minister in Lancashire, regularly counsels youngsters caught in the grip of the occult. He believes that there are 30 witches covens in the North East of Lancashire alone.

Clive Manning says, "Ouija boards, tarot cards and other such things are far from harmless. If you are prepared to try and contact forces outside of yourself, then of course this is possible.

Many of these activities, including palmistry and astrology, can be like conveyor belts. Once you are on them you cannot get off, they are not a game, they are highly dangerous."

"One of the innocent faces of the occult is spiritism. There are around 52,000 spiritists in Britain compared with nearly eight million Christian Church goers *(these figures have altered today)*. Yet the nation's attention is regularly captured by those claiming to bring messages from beyond the grave."

"Medium Doris Stokes became a national celebrity. Her paperbacks sold millions and she could sell out the London Palladium in 24 hours. Britain's spiritist churches and meetings report a 100% growth in attendance in the last five years."[4]

False Cults or Religions

A false religion is any which denies or ignores Jesus Christ as the only Lord and Saviour of the world and the only One who can forgive sins and give us eternal life.

Salvation is found in no-one else, for there is no other name under heaven given to man by which we must be saved.

(Acts 4:12)

Jesus answered, "I am the way and the truth and the life. No-one comes to the Father except through me.

(John 14:6)

Here are but a few that deny or ignore Jesus Christ as Lord and Saviour: Jehovah's Witnesses, Mormonism, Moonies, Christian Science, Scientology, Rajneesh, Yoga and Yoga exercises *(part of Hindu worship)*, Reincarnation, Eastern Meditation, Hinduism, Islam, Buddhism.

The bible warns us not to contact occult powers or seek any supernatural experience outside of Jesus Christ. We are told not to look into the future without His initiative or contact any spirit other than the Holy Spirit, because to do so, always brings evil upon us. We have no right to look into the future, for the future has nothing to do with us. We are told to live by faith in Christ Jesus and not in what we know.

When we touch tar, no matter how lightly, some of it sticks. Many people – and this includes Christians – are suffering mental or physical illness through contact with the occult, at some time in their life.

Fear, obsessions, insomnia, depression, sickness and strong immoral or suicidal impulses can also come on us because of the involvement of our parents and relatives in the things of the occult.

The following are some things to keep clear of:

- **Spiritualism:** Seances, mediums, clairvoyants, natural or spiritual healing groups
- **Fortune telling:** Horoscopes, astrology, psychometry, palm and tea leaf reading, crystal ball gazing, ouija boards, tarot card reading
- **Witchcraft and magic:** Any form of magic, black or white witchcraft *(there is no such things as good witchcraft, it is all from Satan and it is all evil)*
- **Occult objects:** Charms, talismans, fetishes, corn dollies, dream catchers, etc.

- **Psychic practices:** ESP, mind reading, astral projection, automatic writing, levitation, spoon bending, water dividing, table lifting
- **Hypnosis:** For any reason, including medical

❖

CHAPTER 14

Our Response to the Gospel

If you have been involved in any of the above practises in the last chapter then the only way to be free from any interference by Satan is to renounce that involvement. I suggest you go to a brother or sister, church leader and ask them to pray with you.

You need to ask the Lord to forgive you for the sin that you have committed, then renounce Satan and all influence of the occult.

Then the person praying with you can take authority and command any influence that the spiritual forces have inflicted, to be bound and cast out. This will bring healing and the freedom which Jesus intended.

If it is impossible to do the above, follow carefully the next four steps:

1. Destroy all occult objects:

There are many passages in the bible which, tell us it is vital to totally destroy everything to do with occult practices, whether charms, jewellery, charm bracelets, books, games and objects, no matter how ancient or valuable *(read Deuteronomy 12:2-3; Acts 19:19).* This also applies to magazines, tapes, records and any special clothing or paraphernalia that have been used.

2. Forgive:

Jesus said that God cannot forgive us until we forgive others *(read Matthew 6:12-15).* If you are to get free and stay free, it is essential to get rid of all unforgiveness and resentment. To hold nothing against anyone. Forgiveness is a decision, not a feeling. Be determined to forgive everyone *(living or dead),* who has ever hurt or offended you. Repent of every bitterness and criticism and ask Jesus to help you to become a loving and forgiving person.

3. Join a Church:

It cannot be over-emphasised how important it is to remain within the protection and care of the Christian family. Find the Church God wants you to belong to, where Jesus, the Holy Spirit and the bible are honoured and then become a loyal and committed member. This is where you will find strength and help whenever you need it.

4. Be filled with the Holy Spirit:

When He directs your life you will find a new and deeper desire to love and worship Jesus, to read His Word and obey Him continually.

These four steps will keep you safely under God's full protection. If you have followed them, you will be well prepared to receive healing and deliverance. The following is a suggested prayer of renunciation, but we recommend that you say this with the help and support of mature Christians whenever this is possible.

"Lord Jesus Christ, I know you died for me on the Cross. You bore all my sins in Your body and shed Your Blood to save and give me eternal life. I know You are Lord of all, and You have absolute power and authority over Satan and every evil spirit and I believe You will set me free right now. I ask You, Jesus to help me forgive all those I have resented and I now forgive each one freely in Your Name and ask Your blessings upon them. Please put Your love for them into my heart.

I believe You have now done this and I thank You Jesus. I confess I have disobeyed Your Word, in seeking wrong supernatural experiences apart from Yourself and I ask Your forgiveness for this. Please help me renounce it all and clean me in my spirit, soul and body, with Your precious Blood." (Name every practice that you remember. Now include any that you know of, in the lives of your relatives).

"In the Name of Jesus I now utterly renounce every one of those things. I hate them and separate myself from them, and I call upon You Lord Jesus, to set me completely free from every evil effect or curse. Thank You, Lord, for doing this, thank You for setting me free."

❖

CHAPTER 15

A Final Word

S atan is out to destroy people, to deceive them, anything to keep them from the truth. He has his fingers in every aspect of today's society, from children's games *(like dungeons and dragons)* to adult games, such as astrology, ouija boards, fortune telling and tarot cards.

Your children playing games like dungeons and dragons may seem like fun to you, but they are being controlled by what they are playing. When they role play they are actually being controlled by the spirit of that role.

Stop Channelling

Many school teachers today have children sitting quietly, they tell these children to imagine themselves in a field surrounded by flowers. It goes on until they meet an imaginary friend.

This is not just harmless fun, they are teaching our children "channelling," how to open themselves up to the spirit realm, your child can actually become heavily influenced by this "imaginary friend," to the extent that they will start talking and having conversations with this "friend," *(who, incidentally, is not a friend but a demon/spirit guide).*

This is not fun, children are being controlled, it's not right, it's not healthy, it is unscriptural and a doorway to the demonic realm.

Many people are rejecting the things of God because of what they want themselves. This rejection is an implication of control. If they were set free, knew His truth, they would automatically want that relationship with God. Isn't this why Jesus came to die on the cross, so that we can have restored, that which is rightfully ours?

We need to have a love and compassion for every brother, sister and unsaved person. Unfortunately, the fact is, we often look at the circumstances, rather than what is controlling people. The spirit of control is dominating people's lives through such things as, poverty, knowledge, free expression, fear, and religion.

I believe if people are filled with the power of the Holy Spirit, He will illuminate the Word, bringing it to life, consequently bringing fresh revelation. It is the revelation of the truth that sets people free.

Then you will know the truth, and the truth will set you free.

(John 8:32)

The truth will set us free from fear and poverty. It is the poverty spirit, the spirit of lack, which is coming against many Christians. For example, there is no spirit of generosity in the Church today because the spirit of greed in the culture and the spirit of poverty are in the Church and strongly influence our lives. We must be free of these influences.

Knowledge that does not bring edification and change is like, "free expression." We need knowledge, we need the Word, but it must be the "Rhema Word." The "Rhema Word" brings life not just knowledge.

Free Expression is Questionable

There is a whole movement today called, "free expression," where there is no accountability or discipline. Liberals are trying to change the laws, so that parents will not be allowed to discipline their own children. This is unscriptural! You can take anything to the extreme of course. We are not told to "beat" our children but we are told to discipline and nurture them.

> *A refusal to correct is a refusal to love; love your children*
> *by disciplining them..*
> (Proverbs 13:24 MSG)

If you want spoilt children, *(overindulged, narcissistic and rebellious)*, then refuse to discipline them! Delinquent parents *(who refuse to take responsibility even when it is uncomfortable)*, raise delinquent children. Letting them do whatever they want, does not gain their respect. On the other hand, disciplining our children *(in the spirit of love, nurture and respect)*, helps them to grow up into secure individuals; where they generally adjust better and possess a healthier understanding of right and wrong.

This goes against the philosophies of the world. People are teaching that it is harmful for parents to discipline their own children. They are getting completely confused with the issue of child abuse. Disciplining your own children is not child abuse.

Discipline done through love and nurture leaves a positive impact on a child. Abuse however, leaves a child battered, bruised and mentally afflicted.

Failing to discipline our children at the right age, is a neglect of our parental duties. As Christians, scripture is our pattern:

> *Now to you, children, obey your parents in the Lord because this is right in God's eyes. This is the first commandment onto which He added a promise: "Honor your father and your mother, and if you do, you will live long and well in this land."* **And, fathers, do not drive your children mad, but nurture them in the discipline and teaching that come from the Lord.**
> *(Ephesians 6:1-4 VOICE)*

> *Fathers, don't exasperate your children by coming down hard on them.* **Take them by the hand and lead them** *in the way of the Master.*
> *(Ephesians 6:4 MSG)*

❖

CHAPTER 16

Questions from Students

Question 1: Should we say all sickness has demonic influence? Because I thought that some sickness can come from bad feeding, bad climate and bad odors?

> **Answer:** Not all sickness is from demonic influence. Common sense and good hygiene are good deterrents and obvious contributors to wellness!
>
> [As believers we are not "science deniers" as is often the accusation]. However, consider the fact that gossip and murmuring can produce sickness etc. BUT not everything is because of sin or demons. YET, we do live in a world where there is fallen nature - opposed to heaven where there is no sickness at all.

Question 2: Concerning possession, if the soul of man which is the centre of decisions can be possessed, will he be able to repent? (if his will is chain)?

Answer: For this see Mark 15:1-20 and/or Luke 8. Here is the account of the demon possessed man (legion). Notice how Jesus didn't even attempt to talk to the man. Because he wasn't in his right mind (v15). In fact he spoke to the demons and they spoke to Him. It was only after he was in his right mind that the man spoke to Jesus and Jesus to him.

In other accounts of healings in the bible Jesus would ask the individual (even when blind for example), what they wanted from Him. This implies the exercise of "free will"... etc. But in the case of "possession" (the man with legion) - Jesus did not do that. He cast the demons out, without negotiation, or asking the man anything. He only asked the demon its name. Go and read the account afresh.

Also in the course material I will point you back to the quotation provided by John Wimber:

V. (5) Our Perspective of the Temple

A. I need to re-affirm that I do not believe that a Christian can be Demon Possessed

1. To be possessed means to be completely taken over – spirit, soul and body – by the devil:

I do believe however, that a Christian can be oppressed, remembering that there are degrees of "oppression" and "possession."

162

a) *I will not be discussing whether evil spirits inhabit or invade non-believers; but our attention will be focussed on the question:* **"Can a Christian have a demon?"**

2. John Wimber says:

"A Christian cannot be demon possessed because this implies ownership. We are born of God and have His Spirit living within us.

a) *'Affliction, oppression, bondage, and stronghold,' are words used to describe demonization of a lesser extent. This is much more common. This implies varying degrees of demonic influence in certain areas of a person's life.*

b) *This can be linked to a military invasion of a city - even while the friendly forces occupy and control the city, isolated areas can remain under enemy dominion e.g. a deaf and dumb spirit (Mark 9:25), a spirit of seduction or deceiving spirits (1 Timothy 4:1).*

c) *Christians can be demonized on these levels of influence if they allow themselves to be. 1 Corinthians 10:20-22; 2 Corinthians 10:4-5; 1 Timothy 4:1-3. See 1 John 5:18-19 for the security of the believer"* [Spiritual Warfare with John Wimber (Published by Mercy Publications, USA, 1988) p231].

Please know there is a difference between oppression, affliction and possession. For example we know that "God anointed Jesus of Nazareth with the Holy Ghost and with power: who went about doing good, and **healing all that were oppressed of the devil;** for God was with him" (Acts 10:38 KJV).

163

Again, "oppression" and "possession" are two separate things. Affliction, oppression, torment etc... are not necessarily indicators of full possession. Remember Jesus couldn't talk to the man who was possessed until after his deliverance - because it was pointless - the man's "will" was fully taken over. Jesus knew this, and is why He didn't attempt to talk directly to the man until after his deliverance.

This can be considered full possession - involving ownership. Simply Jesus had mercy on the man. The demons were actually begging Jesus to leave them alone and not torment them! The man did not speak at this point. I repeat, he was fully taken over (mind, will and emotions). But this is not always the case, and when it comes to more superficial affliction, torment and oppression - these manifest in varying degrees.

Why the man came to be "possessed" so severely in the first place, we do not know. The scriptures do not fully reveal this. The fact is, he was and many are today. But many are afflicted in varying degrees. Basically Jesus is the answer to all and His power alone ends all theological debate!

Let me emphasise that being tormented in ones thoughts is vastly different to full possession. And yes sin is involved. Sin opens the door very often. Exposing oneself (or being exposed as a child against your will) to the demonic realm, via many different occult practices or horror movies for example, (but there are many spiritual gateways). Every case is different. People are exposed for different reasons. Some willingly, some ignorantly.

The man possessed by "legion" couldn't talk for himself, but was forgiven anyway! Notice, there was no condition to his deliverance. There was no requirement for him to "repent" before Jesus delivered him. Though repentance is necessary, a man who has lost his mind cannot do so. And in this case we see mercy triumphing over judgment! "For the Son of Man did not come to **destroy** men's lives but to save *them*" (Luke 9:56 KJV).

As ministers we must take Jesus' place to set the captives free, including those who can't speak for themselves:

Remember Proverbs 31:8-9 - "Open your mouth for the speechless, in the cause of all *who are* appointed to die. Open your mouth, judge righteously, And plead the cause of the poor and needy" (NKJV).

Jesus as the eternal intercessor, pleads for the undeserving, He brings them into a place where they have a sound mind and can make right decisions. We too must stand in the gap in this way.

Question 3: I thought that the will of man cannot be influenced (chained) by Satan?

Answer: Depends if we are talking believer or non believer? But in the case of full possession - like the man with legion - then yes. But consider those who dabble willingly with the occult, who choose to "yield" their free "will" experimentally or for fun (for example games such as the "Ouija Board"). Such people who open doors they can't close - are now open to torment - until they get ministry by those who know how - in the church.

Question 4: It's interesting to know that the spirit of man cannot be possession. Sir does that mean a born again Christian if well devoted, can he Deliver himself?

> **Answer:** Self deliverance is important. Something this ministry believes in and has practiced for many years. One must keep themselves, pure, clean and free. The teachings of the bible are clear on this. "Keep thy heart with all diligence; for out of it are the issues of life" (Proverbs 4:23) and prevention is always better than a cure! In other words, we can avoid many an affection, through right-living / through obedience to God's Word / and by being led daily of the Holy Spirit.
>
> As you know - spiritual warfare is very real and sometimes "oppression" will just come upon you - for no reason. Just as a spiritual attack. And you must pray it off. Pray it off your children and spouse for example and keep your family covered. It is our responsibility. Not all oppression is because of sin. Not all sickness is because of sin.

❖

The Character of the Ministry

The particular characteristics of Alan Pateman Ministries International, is that of speaking prophetically, with all boldness, to this generation. To reveal the heart of God in stirring up and drawing forth the dynamic potential that has been deposited in the Church. In so doing, exposing the darkness that has for so long gripped the entire world.

This is not a popular style, but one that mirrors the lives of many who have dared to live the life of Christ in their day. Those who have taken their inspiration and motivation solely from the Word of God and backed it by the power and might of the Holy Spirit. "The Word of Life" gives no comfort or consolation to the "flesh." The regenerated spirit however, loves it!

God is challenging everything that can be challenged. This is the "Joshua Generation," the time for the Church to rise up, take its position in the heavenlies with Christ Jesus and to possess the land before it.

It is not a time to wander around and die in the wilderness or be maintained and fed like infants. It is the time for the mighty men and women of valour to rise, run to the battle and then having done all, to stand firm against every power of evil that exalts itself against the knowledge of Christ.

It is a time of BOLDNESS not timidity; a time for STRENGTH not weakness; a time for FERVENCY not ease; and a time for a mighty demonstration of the love of God towards all mankind in DELIVERANCE and PROSPERITY. In all, a time of restoring the righteousness of the Blood Covenant of Jesus Christ.

The Testimony of Jesus is the spirit of Prophecy (Revelation 19:10).

Jesus received witness from and bore witness to, the spirit of prophecy upon John the Baptist. John was outstanding in his refusal to compromise the truth. He was outspoken, eccentric in appearance and lifestyle. He was received by those who hungered after God and rejected by the religious and governmental authorities. He was fearless and bold and of him Jesus said no greater man had ever been born of a woman!

His voice was the voice that heralded the coming of the only begotten Son of God. The lonely Elijah's voice, *"The voice of the one crying in the wilderness."* He was the one who ploughed up the ground to receive the seed of Jesus Christ, he prepared the way. He had a necessary work to do, without which the ministry of Christ could not have been fulfilled.

For Christ to come, the voice of the prophet had to be heard. The ministry of the prophet had to come forth. *"The testimony of Jesus is the spirit of prophecy."* Just as Jesus declared of John that no greater one had ever been born of a woman, so it will be again. The voice of the prophetic that ushers in and heralds the return of the Lord Jesus Christ, will be the greatest prophetic voice ever heard! It will have the roar of a lion and carry the demands of all righteousness.

Since the times of Martin Luther, five centuries ago, when God restored the truth of salvation being by grace and of justification by faith, there has been a progressive period of revelation and restoration given to the Church.

The Protestant Movement was followed by an awareness of the need for water baptism, sanctification, divine healing, the baptism of the Holy Spirit, prophetic presbytery *(church government, apostolic ministries etc.)* and then by the Charismatic Movement, which brought every member of the Body of Christ to the edge of the promised land.

Now is the time to take the cities. To take the land with a shout! The combined anointing of Joshua and David has been released. The anointing of the "Warrior" and "Worshipper," the Deliverer and King. This has to be the most exciting and privileged time to live in. To be able to see with the eyes of the Spirit both all that has passed and that which is to come. The Church, the Bride of Christ, will leave this planet in triumph, not defeat. It will seem to be just like John the Baptist, whose life was cut short. His job was complete. So also will be the work of the Church and Her prophetic voice.

> *See, I will send you the prophet Elijah before that great and dreadful day of the Lord comes.*
>
> *(Malachi 4:5)*

BOLDNESS, STRENGTH, FERVOUR, WISDOM, REVELATION, COMPASSION, LOVE and HUMILITY with EXCELLENCE are the hallmarks of, "Alan Pateman Ministries International," through prayer, worship, witness, spiritual warfare and every other aspect of ministry!

> *The Kingdom of God suffers violence, and the violent take it by force.*
>
> *(Matthew 11:12 NKJV)*

❖

Endnotes

Dedication

1. Ian Andrews, www.iequippers.org, www.citadelministries.com, Equipped to Heal, Published by Onwards and Upwards, 2010, ISBN-13: 978-1907509179

Chapter 1 His Origin

1. Spiritual Warfare (page 53), by John Wimber, Published by Mercy Publications, 1988

Chapter 3 Ruler of the World

1. Christian Set Yourself Free, by Graham & Shirley Powell, Published by New Wine Press, 1986

Chapter 4 Heavenly versus Demonic Music

1. Bands, Boppers and Believers, by Rob Mackenzie, Titles Distributed by Crossroads in Australia (September 1987), ISBN-13: 978-0620108829

2. Cosmopolitan Magazine (page 73), September 1986

3. Bands, Boppers and Believers, by Rob Mackenzie, Titles Distributed by Crossroads in Australia (September 1987), ISBN-13: 978-0620108829

4. Preaching and Preachers by Dr Martyn Lloyd-Jones, as quoted in Pop Goes the Gospel, John Blanchard, page 17

5. San Francisco Chronicle (page 26), April 13, 1966, as quoted in the Legacy of John Lennon

6. Set the Trumpet to Thy Mouth (page 92), by David Wilkinson, Published by Whitaker House, 1993, ISBN-13: 978-0883683187

7. Copies of this tract may be obtained from: Regency Manor, Dollingstown, Craigavon, BT66 7JG, Northern Ireland

Chapter 8 The Passover

1. Life in the Overlap (page 52), by Jean Darnall, Published by Marshall Pickering, 1985, ISBN-13: 978-0551007864

Chapter 10 Our Perspective of the Temple

1. Spiritual Warfare (page 231), by John Wimber, Published by Mercy Publications, 1988

Chapter 12 Entry Points for Demonic Influences

1. Defeated Enemies (page 9), by Corrie ten Boom, Published by Christian Literature Crusade, Fort Washington, Pennsylvania 19034, USA, 2002, ISBN-13: 978-0875080215

2. Sexual Madness, In a Sexually Confused World, by Doctors Alan and Jennifer Pateman, ISBN-13: 978-1-909132-02-3, available from Amazon and other retail outlets: https://www.amazon.co.uk/Alan-Pateman/e/B00JHVDBPO

3. From Curse to Blessing, by Derek Prince, Published by Derek Prince Ministries, P.O Box 300, Fort Lauderdale, FL 33302, USA, 1986

Chapter 13 Involvement in Occult Practices

1. Possess the Land, by Carroll Thompson, Published by Carroll Thompson Ministries, P.O. Box, Dallas, Texas, 75224, USA, 1995

2. Doorway to Danger, Published by the Evangelical Alliance, Copyright E.A. 1987 by CPO, Worthing

3. (ANSA) - Vatican City, February 22, http://www.ansa.it/english/news/vatican/2018/02/22/exorcist-requests-triple-in-italy_a325e0c0-b757-4948-96ca-837b69b50a93.html

4. Doorway to Danger, Published by the Evangelical Alliance, Copyright E.A. 1987 by CPO, Worthing

Endnotes

Bible translations

- Unless otherwise indicated, all scriptural quotations are from the HOLY BIBLE, NEW INTERNATIONAL VERSION ®. NIV ®. Copyright © 1973, 1978, 1984 by the International Bible Society. Used by permission of Zondervan Publishing House. All rights reserved.

- Scripture references marked KJV are taken from the King James Version of the bible.

- Scripture references marked MSG are taken from The Message. Copyright © 1993, 1994, 1995, 1996, 2000, 2001, 2002. Used by permission of NavPress Publishing Group.

- Scripture references marked NKJV are taken from the New King James Version®. Copyright © 1982 by Thomas Nelson, Inc. Used by permission. All rights reserved.

- Scripture quotations marked VOICE are taken from The Voice™. Copyright © 2008 by Ecclesia Bible Society. Used by permission. All rights reserved.

❖

Ministry Profile

Doctor Alan Pateman, an apostle, is the President and Founder of **"Alan Pateman Ministries International"** (APMI), which was established in England back in 1987, a Christian-based *(parachurch)* non-profit and non-denominational outreach. This ministry is now focusing in two main areas: First **"Connecting for Excellence"** Apostolic Networking (CFE) and secondly, the teaching arm, **"LifeStyle International Christian University"** (LICU).

CFE is a multi-facetted missions organisation with the purpose of connecting leaders for divine opportunities and building lasting relationships, to touch the lives of leaders literally the world over. Apostle Dr Alan Pateman has to date ordained more than 500 ministers in over 50 NATIONS. In addition there are ministries, churches and schools who are in Association or Affiliation, looking to him for apostolic counsel and oversight.

Secondly LICU, which was founded in 2007, is a study program to help people discover their purpose and destiny. A global network of university campuses and correspondence students, demonstrating the Supernatural Kingdom of God through Doctrinal, Apostolic and Prophetic Teaching. Dr Alan holds the position of President/CEO, Professor of Theology, Biblical Studies and Apostolic Ministry. LICU is exploding throughout Europe, Asia and Africa, enhancing the Body of Christ

Dr Alan has authored more than 35 books including numerous teaching materials and LICU university courses (30) along with hundreds of Truth for the Journey articles on kingdom lifestyle *(that are regularly distributed globally via the internet).*

He is recognised as an Apostle, Bishop, Leadership Mentor, University Educator, Motivational Speaker, Connector and Author, who has also been featured on national and international TV and radio networks throughout the years.

Currently Apostle Alan, his wife Dr Jennifer reside in Lucca *(Tuscany)* Italy and travel out from their Apostolic Company.

- Alan Pateman Ph.D., D.Min., D.D., M.A., B.Th.

Academic Background

Dr. Alan Pateman attended several colleges throughout his training *(including studying Theology at Roffey Place, Horsham, UK and a Member of Kerygma - with Rev. Colin Urquhart and Dr. Bob Gordon - 1985-1987)* before being awarded a Doctorate of Divinity *(2006)* in recognition of his lifetime achievements by the International College of Excellence, now "DanEl Christian College" *(President: Dr. Robb Thompson USA)* also "Life Christian University" *(Dr. Douglas Wingate USA)* where he also earned a Bachelor of Theology B.Th. *(2006),* a Master of Arts in Theology M.A., a Doctor of Ministry in Theology D.Min., *(2007)* and Doctor of Philosophy in Theology Ph.D. *(2013)* from LICU.

❖

To Contact the Author

Please email:

Alan Pateman Ministries International

Email: apostledr@alanpateman.com
Web: www.AlanPatemanMinistries.com

*Please include your prayer requests
and comments when you write.*

❖

Other Books

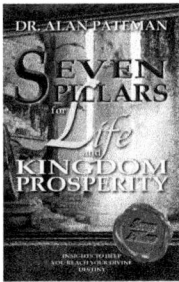

Seven Pillars for Life and Kingdom Prosperity

I submit these "Seven Pillars for Life and Kingdom Prosperity" to you, (Love, Prayer, Righteousness, Obedience, Connections, Management, Money). It's my desire that you walk in the triumphs that God has ordained for you.

ISBN: 978-1-909132-46-7, Pages: 220,
Format: Paperback, Published: 2016
Also available in eBook format!

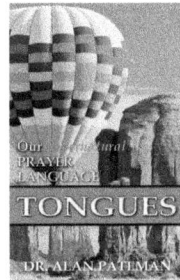

TONGUES, Our Supernatural Prayer Language

In writing to the church at Corinth, Paul encouraged them to continue the practice of speaking with other tongues in their worship of God and in their prayer lives as a means of spiritual edification. "He that speaketh in an unknown tongue edifies, charges, builds himself up like a battery."

ISBN: 978-1-909132-44-3, Pages: 144,
Format: Paperback, Published: 2016
Also available in eBook format!

Truth for the Journey Books

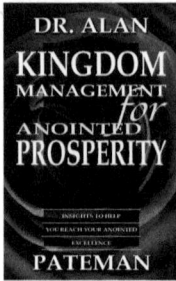

Kingdom Management for Anointed Prosperity

In his book, "Kingdom Management for Anointed Prosperity," Dr. Alan Pateman reveals how we can avoid living in continual crisis due to mismanagement. Life happens to all of us, but how we handle it matters most. "Well done, good and faithful servant! You have been faithful with a few things; I will put you in charge [as manager] of many things. Come and share your master's happiness!" (Matthew 25:21)

ISBN: 978-1-909132-34-4, Pages: 144, Format: Paperback, Published: 2015
Also available in eBook format!

Seduction & Control: Infiltrating Society & the Church

This book is a glance into the world of seduction and control, how they try to influence the Church through many powerful avenues such as the New Age, sexual education in our schools, basic entertainment; things that touch our everyday lives in order that we effectively and gradually become desensitised.

ISBN: 978-1-909132-00-9, Pages: 156
Format: Paperback, Published: 2015
Also available in eBook format!

His Faith Positions us for Possession

It is with both simplicity and seasoned proficiency that Dr. Pateman draws us into this weighty conclusion; ...only as we yield and surrender to Christ's faith IN us – will we truly be empowered to live as Christ lived on this earth, "...as he is, so are we in this world" *(1 John 4:17).*

ISBN: 978-0-9570654-0-6, Pages: 128, Format: Paperback, Published: 2014
Also available in eBook format!

Truth for the Journey Books

WINNING by Mastering your Mind

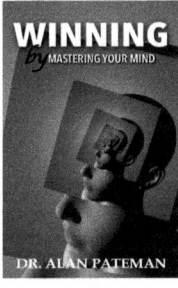

Someone once said, "Happiness begins between your ears and your mind is the drawing room for tomorrow's circumstances..." Remember, what happens in your mind will happen in time, and therefore one of our first priorities must be mind-management.

ISBN: 978-1-909132-40-5, Pages: 136,
Format: Paperback, Published: 2017
Also available in eBook format!

Sexual Madness: In a Sexually Confused World

This book discusses the sensitive subject of political correctness in our world today and the growing fear of causing offence in the public arena. It also discusses the rise of homosexuality, pedophilia and all other forms of sexuality, as there are many. Including modern statistics on pornography.

ISBN: 978-1-909132-02-3, Pages: 160,
Format: Paperback, Published: 2012
Also available in eBook format!

Millennial Myopia, From a Biblical Perspective

The standard for every generation is Jesus. However Millennial Myopia describes the trap of focusing everything on one particular generation or demographic cohort, at the exclusion and expense of all others. The Church cannot afford to make this mistake too. Loaded with research, this book takes readers on a journey of discovery, revealing the true nature of kingdom diversity.

ISBN: 978-1-909132-67-2, Pages: 216,
Format: Paperback, Published: 2017
Also available in eBook format!

Dear Friends,

Have you considered becoming one of our international students? We are privileged to welcome you, from around the world, to "LifeStyle International Christian University" *(the teaching arm of Alan Pateman Ministries International)*. **An English speaking university** dedicated to your success; to see you trained and equipped to fully succeed in your God given Destiny.

It is our passion to raise up the leaders of tomorrow, who will have influence in all realms of authority, including the Body of Christ. Men and women of strategy, wisdom and true godliness, who'll stand with stature and maturity in this hour.

It's undeniable that in today's world, recognised education has become indispensable, therefore it is our desire to offer well balanced and well structured courses. Those that have been written by gifted and talented ministers of God, who seek to be inspired by God's Holy Spirit.

Consequently we have put together a **flexible curriculum,** designed both for correspondence students and campuses, which is a strategy to reach the distant learner; whether provincial, national or international. In fact we have many correspondence students from around the world, including a growing number of successful campuses, in various countries.

This is a growing platform, where men and women of dignity and passion, can grow and be established in their God given endeavours. As God is the healer of the nations, we pray and believe that many of our alumni will go on to **become world changers** in their own right.

We are proud of each and every one of our LICU students.
It would be our pleasure if you would join them on this incredible journey!

Doctor Alan Pateman

Alan Pateman Prof. Ph.D., D.Min., D.D., M.A., B.Th.
PRESIDENT AND CEO
www.licuuniversity.com www.cfeapostolicnetwork.com
Email: info@licuuniversity.com   Mob: +39 366 329 1315

For more information visit our website/facebook or contact our office, using the details below:

Website: www.licuuniversity.com
Facebook: www.facebook.com/LICUMainCampus
Email: info@licuuniversity.com
Telephone: +39 366 329 1315

Partner
with us

TODAY!

We are looking to impact the world with the gospel, together we can do more! Join with us to equip the Body of Christ through our Apostolic Network, LICU university program, campuses, associated schools, missions, conferences, television programs, publication of articles and Truth for the Journey books.

You can become an APMI FOUNDATION PARTNER with a regular contribution of any amount, whether it is once a month or once a year.

- Receive monthly newsletters
- Connect with partners and leaders at our Connecting for Excellence international meetings
- Partners Dinners
- Personal availability for mentoring by Doctor Alan
- Enjoy complimentary books by Doctors Alan and Jennifer
- For those who GIVE EVERY MONTH £10, £15, £20, £30 or more will save money with special discounts on products, hotel rooms, conferences, and more

Partner With Us Today!
Call Italy: +39 366 3291315
Email: partners@alanpatemanministries.com
www.AlanPatemanMinistries.com

All Books Available

at

APMI PUBLICATIONS

Email: publications@alanpateman.com
*Also Available from Amazon.com
and other retail outlets.*

*If you purchased this book through Amazon.com
or other and enjoyed reading it, or perhaps one of
my other books, I would be grateful if you could
take a couple of minutes to write a Customer
Review, many thanks.*

www.ingramcontent.com/pod-product-compliance
Lightning Source LLC
Chambersburg PA
CBHW071531040426
42452CB00008B/966